Cumberland : June 2002

DEM●S

Demos is an independent think tank committed to radical thinking on the long-term problems facing the UK and other advanced industrial societies.

It aims to develop ideas – both theoretical and practical – to help shape the politics of the twenty-first century, and to improve the breadth and quality of political debate.

Demos publishes books and a regular journal and undertakes substantial empirical and policy oriented research projects. Demos is a registered charity.

In all its work Demos brings together people from a wide range of backgrounds in business, academia, government, the voluntary sector and the media to share and cross-fertilise ideas and experiences.

For further information and
subscription details please contact:
Demos
The Mezzanine
Elizabeth House
39 York Road
London
SE1 7NQ
email: mail@demos.co.uk
www.demos.co.uk

D1354025

System Failure

Jake Chapman

DEM⊙S

First published in 2002 by
Demos
The Mezzanine
Elizabeth House
39 York Road
London SE1 7NQ

ISBN 1 84180 044 9
Typeset by Discript Ltd

Contents

Acknowledgements

Although the ideas presented in this article will be new to most readers they have a long history of development and application. I first came into contact with them through my involvement with teaching Systems to undergraduates at the Open University. I would like to thank all my colleagues there for their contributions to both my education and the development of the ideas over the last 20 years. Particular thanks go to Ray Ison, Dick Morris, Chris Blackmore and Tony Wright for their comments on drafts of this article. I am also indebted to John Hamwee and Peter Roberts both for their comments on drafts and their wisdom when it comes to systems thinking. I am also extremely grateful to Nigel Edwards and Paul Plsek for inspiring conversations – particularly regarding how systems ideas could be used in the NHS. The NHS examples were suggested by Nigel Edwards and his colleagues. The idea for this article arose in a conversation with Geoff Mulgan as a result of attending a Systems conference at the Open University. However it could not have been brought to fruition without the guidance and thoughtful inputs from Tom Bentley and Eddie Gibb at Demos. Notwithstanding the collective wisdom of all these colleagues any errors remaining in the text are entirely my responsibility.

Jake Chapman
April 2002

Foreword

This report offers a solution to a real mystery in health policy in the UK and elsewhere. Why is that good individual policies, based on strong values and even common sense, often lead to disappointing results? Or worse, they produce unexpected adverse effects, as the NHS case studies in this publication show.

The initial response to this dilemma is to try more command and control, better policy making, tough inspection and more standards. When this doesn't work the opposite approach is tried. In different parts of the world health care systems are busily copying approaches from other services that are in the process of abandoning them.

The NHS is too often treated as an organisation which, though complicated, just needs better solutions and clearer thinking. An army of commentators is ready to provide these solutions, ranging from the trite 'bring back matron and get rid of bureaucrats', to the more adventurous but equally simplistic 'privatisation, social insurance and opting out' school.

Apart from the fatal error that their treatment is generally not based on a diagnosis, these commentators suffer from the same problem as many policy makers. The mental models they use to think about policy are inadequate because the NHS is not merely complicated, it is *complex*. That means the relationship between cause and effect is uncertain, and there may not even be agreement on the fundamental objectives of the organisation.

This complexity is found at the level of the clinical team, trust and the NHS as a whole. In a complicated system it is possible to work out solutions and plan to implement them. This is not possible in complex systems where policies and interventions have unpredictable and unintended consequences. As the NHS has shown, complex systems also have remarkable resilience in the face of efforts to change them.

An approach based on an understanding of complexity and systems thinking would allow much more diversity and experimentation. We would become more comfortable with the idea of *emergent strategy*, rather than detailed plans and timetables backed up with a range of special measures for failure. This means that a new road map for policy making and management is required. It also requires courage on behalf of policy makers and the development of a new narrative to explain the process to the public.

Many people in the NHS intuitively understand the need for this change, but until recently there has not been a language to articulate this new approach. This paper begins to answer the question of why bad things happen to good policies, and suggests some ways that policy makers, managers and local leaders could deal with complexity.

Nigel Edwards
Policy Director, NHS Confederation
Visiting Professor London School of Hygiene & Tropical Medicine

Executive Summary

1. The current model of public policy making, based on the reduction of complex problems into separate, rationally manageable components, is no longer appropriate to the challenges faced by governments and changes to the wider environment in which they operate. Key changes include:

   - Increased complexity brought about by the impact of communication technologies and the resulting growth in interactions between the various organisations and agencies
   - A more diverse range of organisations involved in public service delivery, most of them not answerable directly to or under the control of ministers
   - Blurring of the boundaries between domestic and international policy, as a result of globalised communications networks and the liberalisation of economic activity, meaning that events at home are increasingly influenced by international factors, and vice versa.

   The combined effect of this increased complexity is to make it even more difficult to predict the outcomes of policy intervention, especially in systems which do not behave in straightforward, linear ways.

2. The ways in which the current policy model is likely to fail are predictable using a group of ideas and disciplines linked to the study of complex systems; they include unintended consequences, alienation of professionals involved in delivery, and long-term failure to improve overall system performance. If public policy fails to deliver improvements, the electorate will become more cynical about the

ability of politicians to deliver on their promises. These kinds of failure are apparent, and increasingly recognisable, across the range of government policy.

3. **Systems thinking,** which treats public services as **complex adaptive systems,** offers an alternative route to developing solutions and increasing system performance. Systems ideas have developed over the last half century, beginning with operational research, cybernetics and general systems theory. Systems thinking is holistic and deals with complexity by increasing the level of abstraction, rather than seeking to divide the problem into manageable, but separate, elements.

4. Systems ideas are most appropriate when dealing with 'messes': problems which are unbounded in scope, time and resources, and enjoy no clear agreement about what a solution would even look like, let alone how it could be achieved. The ideas most relevant to public policy are those associated with complex adaptive systems, soft systems approaches and developing learning systems for improving performance.

5. One way to visualise the difference between the mechanistic, linear approach to policy and the holistic, systemic approach is to compare the results of throwing a rock and a live bird. Mechanical linear models are excellent for understanding where the rock will end up, but useless for predicting the trajectory of a bird – even though both are subject to the same laws of physics. To the degree that social and organisational systems, like the NHS, show adaptive behaviours they are better regarded as similar to live birds than lumps of rock.

6. A key insight from systems theory is that different individuals and organisations within a problem domain will have significantly different perspectives, based on different histories, cultures and goals. These different perspectives have to be integrated and accommodated if effective action is to be taken by all the relevant agents.

7. This insight conflicts directly with the command and control culture that dominates government and public administration. The use of command and control inevitably fails within complex systems, and alienates people by treating them instrumentally.

8. Although there are many different schools of systems thinking they all agree that when dealing with complex systems the best

approach to improving performance is to take a range of actions, evaluate the results and subsequently learn what works best. This evolutionary approach to learning requires both innovation (variety of actions) and effective feedback on the results of previous actions (a selection process).

9. There are significant obstacles to learning within the process of government and policy making. The most important are:
   - an aversion to failure, exacerbated by the political process which uses failures to score points rather than learn lessons
   - the pressure for uniformity in public services
   - shared assumptions between civil servants and ministers that command and control is the correct way to exercise power
   - lack of evaluation of previous policies
   - lack of time to do anything other than cope with events
   - a tradition of secrecy used to stifle feedback and learning
   - the dominance of turf wars and negotiations between departments, effectively making end-user performance secondary to other considerations
   - the loss of professional integrity and autonomy under the knife of efficiency in policy making, and resistance and protection of vested interests by some professional and intermediary bodies.

   In order for a systems approach to be feasible within government it is essential that learning is prioritised, by tackling these obstacles to some degree.

10. Systems practice is characteristically different from the command and control approach in that
    - interventions would be based upon learning what works, on an ongoing basis, rather than specifying targets to be met.
    - the priority would be to improve overall system performance, as judged by the end-users of the system not just by Ministers or civil servants
    - the policy making process would focus on the processes of improvement, rather than the control of the agencies involved
    - engagement with agents and stakeholders would be based more upon listening and co-researching rather than on telling and instructing. Responsibility for innovation and improvement would be widely distributed

- implementation would deliberately foster innovation and include evaluation and reflection as part of the overall design.

11. From a systems perspective an ideal policy statement would consist of a **minimum specification** with the following ingredients:

    a) clearly establish the **direction** of change

    b) **set boundaries** that cannot be crossed by any implementation strategy

    c) **allocate resources**, but without specifying how they should be used. This should also include statements of time scale and potential further funding

    d) **grant permissions** i.e. explicitly allows innovation

    e) **specify core evaluation requirements**, in all cases based upon the experiences and outcomes of the end users of the system.

12. Government and policy makers should begin to experiment more widely with systems methods in investigating a range of public policy 'messes'. The plethora of new strategy and innovation units across central government is in danger of being marginalised unless they can find new ways of working across existing departments and encouraging new ways of viewing existing problems. Scaling up systems approaches, and building them into career development and training for policy makers and other public servants, should be a priority.

13. Systems thinking predicts that individuals will not change their mode of thinking or operating within the world until their existing modes are proved beyond doubt, through direct experience, to be failing. In many domains, including science, new ways of thinking tend to become dominant only when the old vanguard die off. It would be a disaster if public policy has to fail catastrophically, or the present generation of politicians and civil servants die out, before systems ideas were adopted by government.

1. Introduction

There is a perceived crisis in the ability of government to deliver improved performance in key areas of public service – particularly crime, education, health and transport. Part of the difficulty is that the recipients of these services, the public, are becoming more aware of their own needs and aspirations and of the inadequacies of the services with which they are provided. Another source of difficulty is the growing disillusionment with government, which to many appears to spend more time putting a positive 'spin' on bad news than on generating genuine progress or good news. At the same time the professions involved in the key public services, teachers, doctors, the police, are becoming more vocal in their objection to government policy, the ever increasing administrative load imposed on them and the loss of quality in their work. In addition to these public issues and disputes, an increasing number of voices are questioning the prevailing approach to policy design and implementation. These range from those who criticise 'control freakery' to those who question the intellectual foundations of policy making. The world has become more complex, more interconnected, more global and less predictable. Thus, it is argued, the traditional mechanistic command-and-control approaches are less tenable and more likely to generate consequences unintended by their designers.

The main aim of this pamphlet is to demonstrate the ways in which systems thinking can make sense of these interconnected issues and provide a new approach to public policy that is more in tune with the modern world. In the long run, this approach may contribute to re-creating government that can be responsive, effective and legitimate in the twenty-first century.

I shall start by making a general case for a more holistic approach to policy, based on systems thinking. The core argument is that the assumptions embedded in the rational and mechanistic approach to policy are no longer valid and that in the more connected, complex and unpredictable world of the twenty-first century a different approach is called for. This general argument is not new, and I quote several authors in support of it. To develop the argument in more detail I shall explain what systems thinking is and introduce its core concepts. If you are not familiar with these ideas the material in the sections that follow may appear dense, but it is essential to the later discussion. As I shall make clear, systems is a mature discipline with many schools of practice, so it will not be possible to convey the full depth of the subject here. My aim is to introduce enough in order to demonstrate its relevance.

Once the core ideas are in place I use systems thinking to predict the outcomes of using the conventional policy making process, which is based on a linear, mechanistic view of how organisations function and can be directed. This leads to the conclusion that a key ingredient missing from much of that process is learning, ie discovering what works by way of action, evaluation and reflection. As well as introducing a systems approach to learning, I discuss a wide range of institutional and conceptual barriers to learning that exist within the policy making process. This analysis clarifies why making changes in it is at least as difficult as making changes in the NHS, the education system or the transport system. I conclude by describing what systems practice applied to public policy would entail and the generic changes that might be expected as a result.

What emerges from this pamphlet is that systems thinking and systems practice do not provide a simple solution to the severe difficulties facing policy makers in many areas. Rather, a systems approach suggests the need for a shift in the goals that can be realistically achieved by policy, and places policy implementation in the context of a learning organisation that ensures its maximum effectiveness. Rather than proposing any sort of panacea or silver bullet for policy, I am suggesting a shift of paradigm for it. This shift will have the benefit of failing less, by combining improved understanding of the issues, more sensitive policies and more effective implementation. It is important to recognise that these benefits are not easily achieved. What I am setting out here is akin to a restaurant menu; but to know what the food actually tastes like you have to *experience* what is on offer – not just read about it. If you are partly persuaded or simply intrigued by the possibilities offered by systems thinking, there is a list of references for further reading and exploration of the subject for you to consult.

2. Current Policy Making

The conventional description of 'rational policy making' has four steps:

1. clarifying objectives (which are assumed to be unambiguous);
2. identifying the alternative means of achieving those objectives (perfect rationality requires that all possible options are identified);
3. identifying the consequences, including all the side effects, of each alternative means;
4. evaluating each set of consequences in terms of the objectives so that the best policy can be selected and implemented.

This process forms part of a general approach, which I describe below as reductionism. This approach attempts to break a problem down into component parts and tackle them in a rational, linear manner in order to solve them. It presumes that the area for which the analysis and intervention are planned can be understood in a fairly straightforward mechanical and linear fashion. This is reflected not only in the assumptions of what can be analysed but also in the language used, the levers of power, policy instruments and so on. As numerous authors[1] have pointed out, the 'rational' model makes unreasonable assumptions about the clarity of objectives and the information available on means and consequences, and is actually rarely followed. However, their critiques have not questioned the implicit linearity assumed between a policy decision, a corresponding intervention and a set of consequences. One of the main insights provided by systems thinking is that in many areas the range of interconnections and feedback makes it impossible to predict, in advance, the detailed consequences of interventions. Indeed, the consequences are often 'counter-intuitive'.

An example of this can be found in the policy widely used to tackle the use of illegal drugs. It has been well established that the use of illegal drugs such as heroin leads to increased crime, by addicts needing to purchase drugs, and to the increased cost of health care for addicts. One widely used policy is to aim to reduce the supply of drugs through increased activity by police and customs officers tackling actual or potential importers and suppliers. If the policy succeeds, then the supply of drugs will be reduced. If the supply of drugs is reduced, then dealers will have to pay a higher price for a smaller quantity; so they will 'cut' the drugs with other chemicals in order to increase their volume and they will also raise the street price of the drugs. The raised street price means that addicts have to steal more to get their daily fix. The increased mixing with other chemicals significantly increases the health hazards associated with drug use. Thus to the degree that this policy succeeds in reducing the supply of drugs it will exacerbate the crime and health problems associated with drug use that it intends to reduce.

This example illustrates a relatively simple feedback operating in a highly complex area. As with all the examples referred to in this pamphlet, there is an inevitable trade-off between making a point succinctly and over-simplifying the issues and area involved. The aim is not to claim superior insight into any particular policy or area of policy but rather to illustrate, as simply as possible, the real difficulties faced by policy makers.[2]

Another example of feedback that has become familiar in recent years is the development of strains of bacteria resistant to antibiotics, apparently resulting from the much greater use of antibiotic drugs to reduce common infections. The result of this form of human-influenced evolution is that prescribing effective drugs for serious infections has become more difficult and that secondary infections picked up in hospitals are becoming increasingly difficult to eradicate, leading to serious problems for policy makers and hospital administrators.

In many domains of public policy, the world in which the policy maker aims to intervene is beyond complete comprehension. The complexity involved precludes the possibility of being able to predict the consequences of an intervention. Under these conditions the linear rational model of policy making fails to guide the policy maker.

What makes prediction especially difficult in these settings is that the forces shaping the future do not add up in a simple system-wide manner. Instead, their effects include non-linear interactions among the components of the systems. The conjunction of a few small events can produce a big effect if their effects multiply rather than add.... It is worth noting that the difficulty of predicting the detailed behaviour of these systems does not come from their having large numbers of components.... For us 'complexity' does not simply denote 'many moving parts'. Instead, complexity indicates that the system consists of parts which interact in ways that heavily influence the probabilities of later events.[3]

Instances of such systems in open, diverse societies abound, and include car use and traffic patterns and the ways economies respond to unexpected shocks. Without the ability to predict the outcomes of policies, the policy maker is confronted with no rational basis for choice and with a growing probability of unintended consequences, most of which will be harmful to the original policy objectives.

The preceding discussion has argued that feedback, non-linearity and complexity all undermine the conventional, 'rational' basis of policy making. These same characteristics support the notion that a more holistic approach is more likely to succeed. However, the claim

---

Unintended consequences, No 1:
How one part of a complex system may lose out as a result of interactions between other parts
In 2001 there was an additional award of £21million to ambulance services for improving their category A performance. This ended up costing the London Ambulance Service £1.5 million. The bulk of it went to services outside the London area whose performance was most in need of improvement. They used the funds to recruit more staff, the bulk of whom were obtained from the London Ambulance Service. In 2001 it lost 75 more staff than it would have done through normal attrition rates. The cost of making good the 75 lost staff is about £20,000 per person, for recruitment and training.

---

that the world is more complex has been made by each successive generation. It could be argued that this is a subjective sense that cannot be used to justify significant changes in the way policy is approached. Is there anything more concrete that supports the perception that the world is becoming more complex?

If complexity is often rooted in patterns of interaction among agents, then we might expect systems to exhibit increasingly complex dynamics when changes occur that *intensify* interactions among their elements. This, of course, is exactly what the Information Revolution is doing: reducing the barriers to interaction among processes that were previously isolated from each other in time or space. Information can be understood as a mediator of interaction. Decreasing the costs of propagation and storage inherently increases possibilities for interaction effects. An Information Revolution is therefore likely to beget a complexity revolution.[4]

The authors of this passage could expand their argument by pointing out that the use of information is itself a source of complexity and unpredictability. This arises because the same communication will be interpreted and received differently by different individuals and organisations, the differences reflecting their different contexts, sensitivities and perspectives. The authors point out that many of the key technologies of the twentieth century – radio, TV, the telephone and now computers and the internet – have had the effect of increasing communication and thereby reducing the barriers to interaction. From this perspective the increase in complexity is both real and explicable.

The increasing purview of globalisation also contributes to the need for a different approach. Issues that were once entirely domestic now have ramifications in several international arenas. Issues in this category include many areas of economic policy, corporate law, many regulations and even drugs policies. Correspondingly there are other issues that were once entirely a matter of external relations that now have impacts on domestic policy. In this category are all the ramifications of EU treaties, international agreements that constrain manufacture or emissions and so on. This increase in both the constraints imposed on policies and their potential consequences generates greater complexity and makes the presumptions of the rational, mechanistic approach untenable. One commentator underlines this point with the observation that 'Blair's core team also under-appreciated the complexity of EU politics – it described it as trying to play "15-dimensional chess" – and the immense investment of time and energy needed to achieve any movement. Complexity and intractability also dogged progress in some other areas such as crime.'[5]

The recognition that new approaches to policy making are required is not novel. In a recent report on policy making,[6] the assessment of 'Why policy making needs modernising' is that

> The world for which policy makers have to develop policies is becoming increasingly complex, uncertain and unpredictable . . . Key policy issues, such as social exclusion and reducing crime, overlap and have proved resistant to previous attempts to tackle them, yet the world is increasingly inter-connected and inter-dependent. Issues switch quickly from the domestic to the international arena and an increasingly wide diversity of interests needs to be co-ordinated and harnessed. . . . Government is asking policy makers to focus on solutions that work across existing organisational boundaries and on bringing about change in the real world.

This report also refers to the importance of 'joining up effectively' and to 'the need to involve and communicate effectively with those affected by policies as well as those who deliver them on the ground'. It finds that most policy makers 'concentrate their time on policy analysis leading to advice to Ministers', leaving too little time for analysing impacts in other areas, developing implementation policies and reflecting on both their experience and the results of previous policy decisions. Policy making is regarded as a reactive process, largely driven by events and the need to deliver results in the short term. Elsewhere the report proposes a model of professional policy making that, among other features, 'takes a holistic view looking beyond institutional boundaries to the government's strategic objectives' and also 'constantly reviews existing policy to ensure that it is really dealing with problems it was designed to solve without having unintended detrimental effects elsewhere'. However, the report does not offer any guidance on *how* these attributes are to be realised.

The factors that undermine the traditional policy approach – feed-back, complexity, interconnectedness and globalisation – exacerbate one other, and form the basis of the argument that a new intellectual underpinning for policy is required. However, it is not just the intellectual basis of policy that is inappropriate in the twenty-first century: moral values and the organisational systems used to deliver policy on the ground are also relevant. In a recent article Tom Bentley has argued:

> one clear implication to emerge . . . [is that] the left must let go of command and control as the primary means of intervention to achieve progressive social ends.
>
> There are two fairly simple reasons for this conclusion. First . . . command and control is a framework unsuited to the complex, unpredictable demands of contemporary organisational life. . . .
>
> The second reason is moral. Command and control systems tend to treat people in instrumental ways, a feature they share with unrestrained market liberalism. They assume a directive model of institutional authority in which the priorities, values and know-ledge held at the centre of an institution or community will shape and control the behaviour of those who make up the wider system. But this assumption does not carry in societies where active consent is needed to achieve most kinds of public good, and where people's freedom of choice and action is often paramount as a cultural and political value. It is incompatible with a progressive politics which makes the fulfilment of human potential one of its overriding priorities.[7]

Thus in exploring a new intellectual approach to policy I shall also be seeking a different approach to its implementation.

Other authors have pointed to a wider set of reasons for developing a new approach to policy. For example, in a recent paper[8] Geoff Mulgan identifies seven factors that increase the relevance of systems thinking. These are:

1. the ubiquity of information flows, especially within government itself
2. the pressure on social policy to be more holistic
3. the growing importance of the environment, especially climate change

4. the connectedness of systems, bringing new vulnerabilities
5. globalisation and the ways in which this integrates previously discrete systems
6. the need to be able to cope with ambiguity and non-linearity
7. planning and rational strategy, which often lead to unintended consequences.

He concludes that 'Out of all these factors has come a common understanding that we live in a world of complexity, of non-linear phenomena, chaotic processes, a world not easily captured by common sense, a world in which positive feedback can play a hugely important role in addition to the more familiar negative feedback that we learn in the first term of economics.' He also recognises that 'so far remarkably little use has been made of systems thinking or of the more recent work on complexity' and that in part this is 'to do with the huge sunk investment in other disciplines, particularly economics.'

If Mulgan and others are correct and the changing policy environment does now require a more holistic approach, then the continued use of the linear, rational, mechanical approach to policy will fail ever more seriously, because its assumptions fail to reflect the way the modern world operates. The increased frequency and severity of policy failure will result in the failure of governments of all complexions to deliver on their promises of improvement. This in turn will lead to increased disillusion with government, as it will be perceived to be unable to make the changes that it promises and that are required by the electorate. In a wide range of core government policies this is precisely the challenge with which the Blair government (and many others) are clearly and publicly struggling. In short, the failure of the process of policy making to adapt to the world in which it is operating undermines the basic premise of government: that it can actually govern. This is what underlies the perceived crisis in the ability of government to deliver improved performance in key areas of public service.

3. Systems Thinking

Systems thinking, in the form of a general theory, emerged in the 1950s. It has led to the development of a wide range of theoretical positions and approaches to practice. It is neither appropriate nor practicable to review this rich field in a way that even approaches comprehensiveness. Instead I shall focus on three aspects. The first will be a set of core ideas that are fundamental to all systems thinking. These will be explained and exemplified with an eye to their relevance to decision making and public policy. The second will be the use of the idea of a complex adaptive system as a rich source of insight into complexity. The third will be an introduction to the approach known as soft systems methodology, an approach that has already found wide use in commercial and public policy areas. These aspects represent the parts of systems thinking that have proved most useful in my own experience as an academic and a business manager and in analysing policy issues. The choice of aspects to focus on is restricted by my own understanding; I do not claim that they are the most relevant aspects of systems thinking for any particular purpose. Where appropriate I reference other approaches.

One of the reasons why people find systems difficult to comprehend is that as an intellectual discipline it is not defined by the subjects or issues to which its ideas may be applied. Subjects such as chemistry, economics and literature have both a defined area of application and a characteristic way of thinking about and analysing that area. Systems is more like history or philosophy: it is an intellectual approach to issues that can apply to a wide range of human experience. This does not mean that systems has some sort of universal application, any more than history or philosophy. Systems thinking is useful for tackling issues that are embedded in complexity, particularly where that includes human activity.

One way to understand systems thinking is to contrast it with the reductionist approach to tackling complexity. Reductionist thinking has been remarkably successful, particularly in developing successful theories and models of the inanimate world when combined with scientific procedures. The essential aspect of the reductionist approach is that complexity is simplified by dividing a problem into sub-problems or lesser components. The process of sub-division is continued until the resulting bits are simple enough to be analysed and understood. The operation of the original complex entity is then reconstructed from the operation of the components. But herein lies a potential problem. What if essential features of that entity are embedded not in the components but in their interconnectedness? What if its complexity arises from the ways in which its components actually relate to and interact with one another? The very act of simplifying by sub-division loses the interconnections and therefore cannot tackle this aspect of complexity.

Systems thinking has an alternative strategy for simplifying complexity, namely going up a level of abstraction. Higher levels of abstraction lose detail, and it is the loss of detail that provides the simplification. Thus when people talk about the behaviour of organisations they are eliminating the rich detail of how individuals or groups within that organisation function. The organisation is at a higher level of abstraction than the departments or individuals within it. But the interconnection of the components is largely maintained in the process of abstraction. Since a core systems idea is feedback, both positive (or self-reinforcing) and negative (or self-correcting), complexity can often appear mysterious because of a rich set of feedback loops between the components. But by retaining the connections and avoiding the tendency to break things down, systems provides a holistic approach to understanding and managing complexity.

In learning about systems thinking it is helpful to differentiate between two broad classes of problem, referred to as 'messes' and 'difficulties'.[9] A difficulty is characterised by broad agreement on the nature of the problem and by some understanding of what a solution would look like, and it is *bounded* in terms of the time and resources required for its resolution. In contrast, messes are characterised by no clear agreement about exactly what the problem is and by uncertainty and ambiguity as to how improvements might be made, and they are *unbounded* in terms of the time and resources they could absorb, the scope of enquiry needed to understand and resolve them and the number of people that may need to be involved. Repairing a car that has broken down, deciding the next move in a game of chess and finding the error in a set of accounts are difficulties. They may be difficult; but as problems they are bounded, and individuals will know when they have found the solution. But devising policies to reduce crime or to increase the performance of the NHS is a mess: there is rarely agreement about where the problem actually lies or where improvements can best be made, and it is subject to high levels of uncertainty. Complexity, ambiguity and uncertainty have the capacity to absorb large amounts of resources. Another difference between these classes of problem is that when the problem is a difficulty, an individual claiming to have the solution is an asset, but when the problem is a mess that individual is usually a large part of the problem!

It is now possible to say more about the relevant area of application of systems thinking. In general, reductionist methods predominate in dealing with difficulties. For example, repairing the computer I am using is best done using a reductionist approach. Reductionist approaches have much less success in dealing with messes (although detailed analyses are often useful in tackling part of the complex of problems involved). Systems thinking, and in particular the soft systems approach, provides a framework that has proved to be successful in tackling messes. Thus for dealing with the issues associated with introducing a new computer system in an organisation a systems approach is best. Many people have had the experience of technical experts using a reductionist approach on this kind of problem, and they have found out just how inadequate that is. It should be emphasised that systems thinking does not solve the mess in the same way that it solves a difficulty. Rather, a systems approach will provide a framework within which most or all of the participants can agree an agenda for improvement or a process for moving forward. This is actually the best that can be achieved when dealing with messes, but it may still appear inadequate to someone wedded to the idea of an instant solution.

Before introducing some core systems ideas, I want to stress how important it is that systems thinking should not be seen as a competitor to reductionist thinking. The two are actually complementary. I have deliberately polarised reductionist and systemic approaches, as well as messes and difficulties, in order that the contrast can be used to clarify the underlying concepts. In practice most problems lie between the extremes of messes and difficulties, and some combination of holistic and reductionist thinking will prove the most useful. In my own experience systems thinking has proved most useful in identifying and illuminating differences in perspective and objectives between different participants. It has also alerted me to contexts and interactions that might have been overlooked within more detailed analyses. Oversimplifying again, I suggest that systems thinking can provide an appropriate context within which detailed analyses can be carried out and interpreted.

4. Core Systems Concepts

The word 'system' itself is a source of difficulty, for both newcomers to the subject and to academics wishing to pin down a widely agreed definition. A system is always taken to refer to a set of elements joined together to make a complex whole.

The justification for using the concept is that the whole is regarded as having properties that make it 'more than the sum of its parts'. This is the everyday language expression of the idea of so-called emergent properties, that is to say properties which have no meaning in terms of the parts which make up the whole. Thus a heap consisting of the individual parts of a bicycle does not have vehicular potential. However, when the parts are linked together in a particular structure to make the bicycle as a whole, which does have the potential to get someone with the ability to ride from A to B, that is an emergent property of the bicycle as a whole. The idea of emergent properties is the single most fundamental systems idea and to use this (and other) systems ideas in a conscious organised way is to do some 'systems thinking'.[10]

It is useful to distinguish three broad areas in which systems ideas are widely used. The first is *natural systems*, as studied by biologists and ecologists, among others. Examples include the human body, frogs, forests and catchment areas. The second is *engineered* or *designed systems*, artefacts that are planned to exhibit some desirable emergent properties under a range of environmental conditions. My computer and car, and nuclear power stations, are examples of engineered systems. The third is *purposeful* or *human-activity systems*, and it is the area of prime interest in this work and to those interested in management in its broad sense. All institutions and organisations fall into this area, including ministries, hospitals, prisons and schools.

An underlying concept of systems thinking relevant to natural systems and human-activity systems is the *adaptive* whole. In addition to having emergent properties, the whole has the ability to withstand changes in its environment. Everyday experience provides many examples of this adaptation, which is what makes systems thinking intuitively attractive. For example, the human body can maintain its internal temperature within a quite narrow range while tolerating a wide variation of external temperature. An institution such as the army has continued to survive in a recognisable form even though the world in which it operates and the technology it uses have changed beyond recognition. Businesses adapt to both long- and short-term changes in their markets, with varying degrees of success.

The development of these ideas leads to the concept of the complex adaptive system, which will be developed below. For now, it should be noted that for systems to be adaptive they require a level of self-organisation, which is usually provided through sub-units which are themselves systems, referred to as sub-systems. Most adaptive wholes can themselves be regarded as sub-systems of larger systems. For example, a person can be regarded as part of a family, which is part of a larger cultural system; a business firm is part of an economy, which is part of the world trading system. Similarly, sub-systems can be regarded as containing further sub-systems. The human body contains organs, which are assemblages of cells that have emergent properties and therefore can be regarded as systems. Thus systems thinking often refers to a hierarchy, or sequence of levels, of systems and sub-systems, all of which exhibit the characteristics of adaptive wholes with emergent properties. Within this hierarchy there must be processes of *communication* and *control* in order for the system to be able to respond adaptively to changes in its environment.

Many of the early attempts to apply systems thinking to management and policy used either engineering systems or natural systems for defining concepts and methods. The biological tradition gave rise to the general systems theory of von Bertalanffy,[11] and the engineering tradition emerged through cybernetics and informed much of the work of Beer[12] and others. However, these approaches assumed that human-activity systems could be identified as clearly as engineered or natural systems, and this has proved to be a source of persistent problems. In retrospect it seems naïve of these early efforts to presume that an expansion of content and disciplines would result in a genuinely more holistic approach. In the terms introduced earlier, adding layers of additional analysis did not assist in dealing with messy problems.

The essential reason why adding disciplines and content does not resolve messy problems is basically similar to the reason why the linear reductionist approach to policy fails: they both presume that it is possible to establish the 'facts' of the situation. As will become clearer as this exposition unfolds, a key feature of messes and difficult policy issues is that there are valid different perspectives on the issue or situation, which interpret information quite differently. The early systems pioneers assumed that the different perspectives were limited to those of different disciplines, but this is not the case. Different perspectives arise as a result of different contexts, different cultures, different histories, different aspirations and different allegiances, either institutional or political.

Unintended consequences, No 2:
A counter-intuitive result

One of the surprising results of the NHS's improving performance is that waiting lists for operations may become, indeed need to become, longer. This arises as a result of the system for giving patients advance notice of impending operations. Most hospitals notify patients of their inclusion on operating lists on a monthly basis. This means that each month a hospital has to send out enough notices to ensure that there is a supply of cases for the coming month for, say, hernia operations.

However, if the time taken for an operation has decreased, owing to increased efficiency within the hospital, then the number of patients who can be operated on each day will increase. This means that the number of people on the monthly allocations list must be increased. Thus as the hospital improves its performance and is able to undertake more operations, so the length of its waiting lists must grow.

It was the failure of the systems engineering approach that led Peter Checkland[13] to develop what has become known as soft systems methodology (SSM) (see Section 8). This approach focuses entirely upon human-activity systems, and starts from the presumption that in this area 'systems are in the eyes of the beholder'. It has turned out to be an extremely productive perspective for dealing with messy problems because it recognises and works with the ambiguity inherent in a situation. The point is that when someone refers to the legal system they are not pointing to anything as clearly defined as a computer system or the nervous system of a frog. Although there is a sense in which the legal system can be regarded as an adaptive whole that displays emergent properties and so on, the precise formulation of this whole depends upon the perspective of the person making the observation. Another way of stating this is that different people will have different perspectives on 'the legal system' and that this will result in the system being attributed with different boundaries, different purposes and perhaps even different properties. For example, there will be differences in the perspectives of judges, prisoners, the police, refugees and politicians when they describe the characteristics and purposes of the legal system. It is precisely the resulting ambiguity that makes tackling 'improvements to the legal system' so problematic but makes the SSM strategy, which embraces ambiguity head on, so successful.

A simple example of ambiguity in defining a human-activity system may make the SSM strategy clearer. In the area of energy policy, 'the energy system' consists of the sources of fuel (oil wells, coal mines etc), the fuel conversion plants (oil refineries, power stations etc) and the ways in which fuel is distributed to end-users (gas pipelines, the electricity grid etc) and all the associated organisations (fuel supply companies, regulators etc). However, if a study of it included an investigation of the impact of energy efficiency improvements, then 'the energy system' would need to be expanded to include the equipment used by the so-called end-users: freezers, boilers, cars and so on. Whether the end-user equipment is inside or outside 'the energy system' is determined by the perspective of the practitioner and the purpose of the study, not by an absolute definition. One of the strengths of SSM is that it provides a rigorous framework for defining 'systems of interest', starting from an explicit statement of the purpose or transformation that each system achieves. This is particularly relevant to policy issues associated with delivering better public services, as it is the goals and perception of the service-users that need to be considered explicitly.

The existence of significantly different perspectives on a problem is a key characteristic of a mess, one that is difficult to incorporate in a linear, rational model of decision or policy making. In their discussion of intractable policy controversies, Schön and Rein[14] argue that a root cause of their intractability is the different frameworks used by participants and policy makers to make sense of the world. Echoing many of Thomas Kuhn's comments on conflicts in science arising from different paradigms the authors argue that

> there is no possibility of *falsifying* a frame; no data can be produced that would conclusively disconfirm it in the eyes of all qualified objective observers. The reason for this is that if *objective* means frame-neutral, there are *no* objective observers. There is no way of perceiving and making sense of social reality except through a frame, for the very task of making sense of complex, information-rich situations requires an operation of selectivity and organisation, which is what 'framing' means.

Elsewhere they state: 'Evidence that one party regards as devastating to a second party's argument, the second may dismiss as innocuous or irrelevant.' This means that it is effectively impossible to establish a rational model of decision making or analysis that would span more than one framework. Bluntly put, all analyses based on a single framework or perspective are politically loaded and never neutral. Thus employing an approach that takes into account different perspectives or different frameworks is not a luxury; it is essential if the proposals that emerge are to have anything approaching widespread support.

Associated with this multiple perspective approach is another systems idea: a trap built into the way an individual thinks. It is often the case that an individual or group will define and think about problems in ways that make them harder to solve. A common way this is done is to blame others for the problem, thereby denying oneself any ability to change the situation. For example, policy makers are prone to blame implementers when things go wrong. However, as Mintzberg pointed out, there is no such thing as a gap between strategy and implementation; there are only policies whose poor design fails to take into account the realities of implementation. One sure sign that someone is in a mental trap is when they find themselves in a situation they have faced before and can only think of doing what they have done before – which they know will not work. Sir Geoffrey Vickers has an illuminating observation about traps:

> Lobster pots are designed to catch lobsters. A man entering a lobster pot would become suspicious of the narrowing tunnel, he would shrink from the drop at the end; and if he fell in he would recognise the entrance as a possible exit and climb out again – even if he were the shape of a lobster. A trap is a trap only for creatures who cannot solve the problem it sets. Man traps are dangerous only in relation to the limitations of what men can see and value and do.... We the trapped tend to take our own state of mind for granted – which is partly why we are trapped.[15]

Being open to other perspectives will often help participants to perceive their own mental traps – never an easy process. One of the qualities of people who are good at systems thinking is that they have greater than usual levels of self-awareness and intellectual openness. This is not accidental; these qualities are essential for success in comprehending more than one perspective on, or framework of, an issue.

5. Systems and Modelling

My first introduction to 'systems' was *Limits to Growth*,[16] a summary of the results of a computer modelling exercise concerned with the future development of the world economy. Using relationships among the major variables, which included population, pollution, resources, capital and land, it purported to show that within the next 50 to 100 years the world system, as we now understand it, would collapse. The book became a best-seller, and formed a strong link in people's minds between systems ideas, computer modelling and predictions of future catastrophe. The style of computer modelling popularised in *Limits to Growth* is known as systems dynamics; it is a generalised method for modelling stocks (the accumulation of things) and flows (the motion of things) at any level of aggregation. It is now a relatively small part of systems methodology.

Although very few systems practitioners are engaged in building computer models or simulations, virtually all systems work does involve modelling – but not with quantitative data and computers. The modelling much more widely employed uses diagrams. Earlier it was stated that systems thinking provides a way of simplifying complexity by going up a level of abstraction and retaining, as far as possible, the interconnections between sub-systems. Diagrams of various types facilitate this mode of abstraction. A diagram illustrates relatively easily a rich level of interconnection, which is difficult for text to convey, as illustrated in Figure 1. Although most professionals are familiar with the use of language and mathematics, using diagrams is somewhat strange. It forces them to adopt a slightly different perspective and way of thinking about issues. Thus diagrams can assist in the process of changing the way an individual perceives and thinks about issues, thereby facilitating the intellectual openness and self-awareness referred to earlier.

Figure 1.
The way in which a diagram can represent interconnections

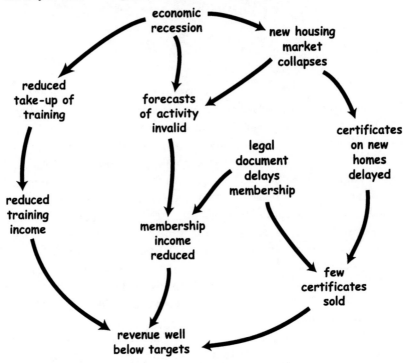

Another example of the use of diagrams comes from soft systems methodology. One of the devices used to capture different perceptions of a messy problem is known as a 'rich picture'. This is a freehand representation of whatever the individual regards as the most salient features of the mess. An example is shown in Figure 2. This type of representation has advantages over the more formal style of diagram illustrated in Figure 1. By making a picture rather than using words most people will express more of their emotional reaction to the mess. This both enhances mutual understanding between those engaged in an SSM project and enables each participant to become more aware of his or her emotional engagement. One of my colleagues was carrying out an SSM day with three members of a company who were negotiating with a developer for the sale of some land. The group was using the SSM day to resolve growing disagreements and friction among them regarding the deal. In his rich picture one of the three participants represented the developer as a very large gorilla intent on destroying the company. This shocked his companions, who did not realise he had this perception. As he was also the person carrying out the detailed negotiations with the developer, it provided them with insight into why they had been falling out over the issue. As my colleague later commented, 'That one picture saved the company many weeks of acrimony and a lot of money!'

Figure 2.
A rich picture from a student case study concerned with the design of Taurus, a computerised stock market settlement system

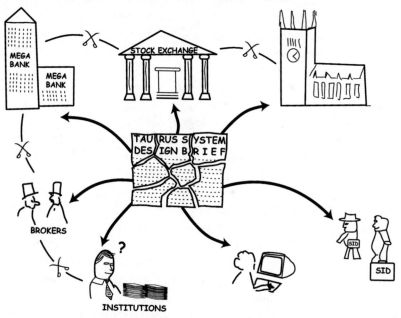

A further example arises from when I facilitated a day-long meeting between the board of a company and its management team. The rich pictures created by the management team all displayed, in different ways, deep conflict, antagonism and despair about the relationship between the company and a particular government department. This was a shock to the non-executive directors, who pointed out that the entire business was driven largely by the various initiatives and legislation that originated from that department. It became clear that the key issue facing the business was how to manage the genuine conflicts while maintaining good relations with the department, which, indirectly, generated most of the company's business. What was needed was to imagine and model a system that would foster a positive relationship between the company and the department. Although this may seem a facile or obvious conclusion, to the participants it was radical; it changed everyone's perspective on what was required. The directors realised that they could assist in reducing the scope of the conflicts, and the managers realised that they needed to temper their desire to 'win' with the need to maintain good long-term relations. The exercise had two important outcomes. First, each individual's perception and understanding was modified. Second, the group of directors and managers as whole now had a common understanding and a greater alignment of objectives, based on conceptualising a common system of interest.

At this point I want to clarify aspects of what a 'system' is. So far I have referred to a wide range of 'systems': the legal system, a computer system, information technology systems at work and now 'a system to foster a positive relationship'. To what degree are these 'real' systems? In order to address this it is useful to introduce a distinction between two broad approaches to systems thinking.

In the systems field there is a distinction between 'hard' and 'soft' systems approaches. This distinction has several dimensions. The first, and most obvious, distinction is in the area in which these approaches are used. The hard systems approach arose from systems engineering and is characteristic of it. This approach usually assumes that the systems themselves are real entities and that the objectives of the system are known and agreed. It usually employs quantitative computer models, using systems dynamics, operational research or similar disciplines, as well as diagrammatic models. In contrast, the soft systems approach arose in applying systems thinking to human-activity systems when there is poor understanding, and even less agreement, about purposes and objectives. Its dominant models are qualitative, and include diagrams and metaphors. However, as Checkland[17] has pointed out, the core distinction between the hard and soft approaches lies not in their subject or the types of model used but in the underlying approach to the identification of systems. In hard systems approaches, the tacit assumption is that a system exists in the external world and may be discovered, designed or otherwise manipulated. In contrast, the soft systems approach assumes explicitly that systems exist only in the eyes of the beholder and are useful mental constructs for dialogue.

It would be inappropriate for this work to attempt to explore or resolve the arguments around the ontology and epistemology of systems, resting as they do on the fundamentally different philosophies of positivism and postmodernism. This is a source of confusion in the systems literature, and will not be resolved, because systems thinking covers all of the natural, engineering and human-activity systems. No matter where one lies on the philosophical spectrum it is always helpful both to be aware of one's underlying assumptions and to communicate these in dialogues that aim to foster greater mutual understanding.

For me, all concepts such as system, institution, organisation, family, group and so on are mental constructs for ordering and making sense of data in the area of human activity. To the degree that they enable me to understand and act appropriately, I shall talk about them *as if* they exist in some sort of external reality. However, as I do not claim that these entities have any *objective* existence, I do my best to remain open to alternative perspectives and constructs. I have found this especially important when moving between different cultures, especially between academic, business and civil service cultures, where concepts and words can carry very different meanings and assumptions. (See the discussion below of stakeholders.) In this sense I do not regard 'system' as having any special ontological or epistemological features. It is just a more fertile source of pluralism because of its comprehensiveness.

6. Complex Adaptive Systems

The main source of understanding the characteristics and properties of complex adaptive systems is observation of natural or living systems. Complex adaptive systems provide a rich source of metaphor in discussing human-activity systems, although some will claim that the latter are also examples of complex adaptive systems. The essential aspect of either approach is that the human-activity system needs to be approached and understood in terms that are quite different from the normal linear, mechanical framework used. This difference has been graphically illustrated by Plsek,[18] who compares throwing a stone with throwing a live bird. The trajectory of a stone can be calculated quite precisely using the laws of mechanics, and it is possible to ensure that the stone reaches a specified destination. However, it is not possible to predict the outcome of throwing the live bird in the same way, even though the same laws of physics ultimately govern the bird's motion through the air. As Plsek points out, one approach is to tie the bird's wings, weight it with a rock and then throw it. This will make its trajectory (nearly) as predictable as that of the stone, but in the process the capability of the bird is completely destroyed. He says that this is more or less what policy makers try to do when using a scientific management approach, based on a mechanical model, to try to control the behaviour of a complex system for which they are devising policy. He also points out that a more successful strategy for getting the bird to a specified end-point might be to place a bird feeder or other source of food at the destination. Here Plsek is extending the metaphor in order to emphasise that influence is possible but that, rather than using control, it is generally more productive to devise strategies that take account of the behaviour and properties of the system involved. In what follows I shall discuss various main characteristics of complex adaptive systems and relate them to the process of making policy. Later I shall draw the various ideas together and derive general conclusions.

A principal feature of a complex adaptive system is its ability to adapt, ie its ability to survive significant changes in its environment through changes in behaviour and internal processes. Adaptation is the process that enables this system to maintain its integrity. But what exactly is it that is maintained? Pursuing this and other questions in the 1960s led the biologist Maturana to develop a deeper understanding of what life is and its relation to cognition and the mind.[19] A core conclusion was that all living things share the same organisation, known as 'autopoiesis'. An autopoietic organisation is a network of production processes in which the function of each component is to participate in the production or transformation of the other components in the network. In this way the entire network continually 'makes itself'. It is produced by its components and in turn produces those components. Although Maturana has always had reservations about the direct applicability of this theory to social or human-activity systems, the parallels have proved irresistible to many theorists.

Regardless of whether human-activity systems can be regarded as autopoietic in the same sense as biological systems or whether autopoiesis is simply a very powerful metaphor, both perspectives point to the fact that many organisations set up internal processes that have the effect of reproducing the organisation over time. What is not in doubt is that institutions and organisations have internal processes that allow them to survive changes in the environment in which they operate. Severe changes to the environment may force an institution to make changes to its staffing levels and organisational tree, but it will remain recognisably the same institution. What is conserved is its internal organisation, core values and culture, and these are conserved by the ways in which 'the right way to do things' are internalised by the individuals within the institution. Anyone familiar with the difficulties of making the transition from public body to private utility faced by the gas, water and electricity companies will know the force of this conservation process.

Viewed from this perspective the resistance to change exhibited by many organisations is not due to the bloody-mindedness of the individuals involved, although that may be a contributing factor. The resistance to change is actually a measure of an organisation's ability to adapt; it is a measure of its resilience. This resilience is therefore expected to be greater the longer the institution has existed and been required to adapt – which is broadly the case. Within all large organisations such as a large firm, a university, a hospital or a government department, there exists 'a network of processes that reproduces itself'. The ways issues are formulated, the terms of reference of committees, the mindsets of the people involved and the network of working relationships between them all serve to keep the existing structures and processes in place. Senior executives, civil servants and vice chancellors who blame the lack of change on the individuals in the organisations they manage have missed the point. If the organisation were unable to change, it would have ceased to exist a long time ago!

Cybernetics, with its detailed description of feedback and control systems, provides another perspective on the adaptive process through the concept of homeostasis. Homeostasis refers to the ability of complex adaptive systems to maintain certain governing variables within defined limits, for example body temperature. While these governing variables are within the prescribed limits, the system can devote resources to other activities. However, if any of the governing variables approaches or exceeds the limit, the system responds by devoting resources to returning that variable to within the limits. This principle can be used to account for the ways in which many organisations, including government, respond to events and other changes in their environment.

For example, in a recent policy exercise in which I was involved, there was a debate about how different policy objectives should be prioritised. The key objectives were economic, social, environmental and security ones. Various participants sought to prioritise one or other of these objectives, but were always defeated by someone else hypothesising circumstances under which another objective would clearly take priority. The debate was resolved by reference to the characteristics of homeostatic systems, namely that the priority given to any objective depends upon how close that objective is to a limit. Thus if all objectives were being satisfied and a new threat arose in regard to, say, social objectives, then the policy process would correctly prioritise social objectives until such time as they were safely within the boundaries or limits regarded as acceptable.

In short the prioritisation of policy objectives is entirely determined by context, which is why the process of policy making, and much else in government, is driven by events (ie changes in context or environment). It should be noted that in policy issues, the perception that an objective is close to a limit depends upon the perspective adopted. This is not as clear as in biological or engineered homeostatic systems.

Considering organisations as complex adaptive systems also challenges the assumptions of causality implicit in reductionist thinking and scientific management. Much of the success of science, technology and scientific management rests on the assumption that it is possible to separate out components and treat their interactions in a linear fashion. This assumption about linearity means that the influence of a change in one part of the organisation can be safely accounted for by evaluating its effects on its immediate neighbours. This also implies that it is possible to explain an outcome in terms of a sequence of causes, ie that A caused B that caused C. Within complex adaptive systems, the dominant mode of response is non-linear. Apparently small changes within a complex system can cause, through feedback and effects multiplying rather than just adding, very large changes elsewhere in the system. Apocryphal examples abound within information technology, where the development of microprocessors revolutionised computing, the first spreadsheet transformed both the personal computer market and management practices, and the first hyper-text browser began the internet revolution. When effects are multiplicative rather than additive, it is not convincing to attribute one change to a single other change.

The richness of interconnections means that any one change has several prior causes and itself may contribute to further changes in these causes. It is precisely in these circumstances that a holistic or systems approach is essential, because the components cannot sensibly be separated, as the reductionist approach assumes. It also means that the behaviour of the system is determined more by its own internal structure than by specific external causes. Furthermore, its own internal structure will have evolved as a result of its particular history, including its previous adaptations to changes in its environment. Here we return to the metaphor of throwing a bird or a stone. With a stone it is sensible to talk about the causes that determine where it ends up; but this is not so with the bird. If one were to throw a live bird, where it would end up would be determined largely by the bird, not by any characteristics of the throw.

This means that to the degree that an organisation can be regarded as a complex adaptive system our normal views of causation are likely to be misleading. This poses a particular problem for policy makers and managers in general. The reason is that the ideas of responsibility and blame are intimately associated with a simple linear theory of causation. If it is true that the behaviour of a university or hospital is determined more by its internal structure and history of development, then how is it possible to hold a vice chancellor or NHS manager responsible when the university produces too few graduates or the hospital treats too few patients? I shall return to this issue later, but for now it should be noted that replacing the vice chancellor or the NHS manager is not, of itself, likely to result in any change in outcome.

Associated with the issue of causation and linearity are issues concerning measures of performance. The dilemma here can be stated simply. In order to provide precision on what is required of managers and to check that progress is being made, it is regarded as essential to provide quantitative measures of performance and targets. Within complex adaptive systems the pursuit of any single quantified target is likely to distort the operation of the system and thereby reduce its overall effectiveness. The dilemma is not hard to understand. What is hard is to find a way out. An instance of this dilemma has been described forcefully in the press:

Last week's report by the National Audit Office on the NHS rightly highlighted how health delivery is disastrously subverted by waiting list targets. The NAO found that to avoid being fined for over-long waiting lists, 20% of consultants 'frequently' ignored clinical priorities in their operations lists, performing simple routine procedures rather than complicated ones in order to make their numbers. What the NAO, like every other outraged commentator, signally failed to point out, however, is that this is a generic problem with all management-by-targets, which is inevitably counter-productive. It systematically lowers quality, raises costs and wrecks systems, making them less stable and therefore harder to improve.[20]

The current government wishes to improve education standards. It has set targets for academic achievements, including new examinations and league tables of results by different schools. But there is difficulty in comparing schools where the culture and entry abilities of the students are markedly different. Also, many teachers have complained that they now have to spend more time on examinations and marking and less on teaching. Finally, it is widely recognised that schools do a great deal more than teach students how to pass examinations and that because these other activities are not included in the measurement of performance and targets they will be neglected. These 'other activities' include sport, learning to socialise, appreciation of art, theatre and music and travel. There is again a real danger that forcing schools to prioritise one aspect of their performance will distort their general performance and thus impoverish the broader education of their pupils.

Unintended consequences, No 3:
How targets can distort overall system performance
In order to improve the treatment of breast cancer, a target was established for urgent referrals. The target required that suspected cases were referred to a specialist consultant within 14 days. There are two ways in which women can be referred to specialists. One is through mass screening programmes; the other is by attendance at a breast clinic run by a specialist consultant. The mass screening programmes are carried out by GPs. They are good at identifying cases with standard symptoms, and for these cases the 14-day targets have improved treatment rates. However, for women with less obvious or hidden symptoms, which GPs are less able to detect, the only route open is attendance at the breast clinic. Here the time to see the specialist has lengthened as a result of the increased referral rate from the general screening programme. As a result, the women with hidden symptoms often end up waiting longer to see the specialist – and their need to see the specialist is greatest.

One of the significant dangers of specifying targets and simple measures of performance is that the result will be sub-optimisation. This is well understood in systems engineering. For example, in the design of operating systems in early mainframe computers,[21] one of the key limitations was the amount of 'core memory' available (equivalent to random-access memory in modern computers). The programmers working on the operating system were therefore given strict limits on the amount of memory they could use, and were encouraged to reduce it even further. The first result was an operating system that ran at a snail's pace. This was because the programmers overcame the memory limit by breaking down their routines into sub-sections that were successively loaded into memory as required, which ensured that they did not exceed their memory budget. But loading the sub-sections into memory was very slow, owing to the technology of the era. And as all the different sub-programs in the operating system were doing the same thing, the whole system was running at a speed determined by the slow loading of the sub-sections. There were other deleterious effects as well, such as programmers achieving their own targets by imposing higher demands on other routines. The message from this, and countless other systems engineering examples, is clear – emphasising a single measure of performance leads to a decrease in overall performance.

The implication for government by targets is clear. Target-setting may be a short-term way to stimulate and focus efforts to improve performance. However, a specific target can encapsulate only one element of a complex organisation, and its dominance is likely to undermine other aspects of the organisation that are crucial to its general and long-term effectiveness. An example would be the apparent link between the ambitious performance targets and heavy measurement in schools policy and the continuous difficulties faced by the school system in motivating and retaining qualified teachers.[22]

To my reductionist colleagues this begs the question of how one defines and quantifies 'overall system performance' if it is not by a single measure of performance. In the case of computers the only way to judge system performance is actually to use the computer in the variety of tasks in which the user is interested. Recognising this, computer magazines that regularly compare different machines and different software products have gone to great lengths to devise tests and measurements, usually involving dozens of separate measures, that can give readers an assessment of the 'overall performance'. In a similar way parents are able to recognise a 'good school', which is not simply one that provides the best examination results. Their assessment will focus on academic achievement, but it will also take into account, often in a qualitative rather than quantitative way, how the school encourages the interests of their child, facilitates adventure, travel, sport and a broad range of experience.

The above arguments suggest that for complex systems, whether engineered or human-activity, the only effective judge of performance is the end-user. This is the basis of the way out of the dilemma associated with measures of performance.

A practical example of avoiding the trap associated with imposing measures of performance on a complex system is the Toyota production system (TPS). This has been described at length by Johnson and Broms,[23] who introduce their main thesis by a quotation from Deming, widely recognised as the originator of the concept of total quality management:

> If you have a stable system, then there is no use to specify a goal. You will get whatever the system will deliver. A goal beyond the capability of the system will not be reached. If you have not a stable system, then there is no point in setting a goal. There is no way to know what the system will produce: it has no capability.[24]

The Toyota production system has been refined and engineered over the past 50 years using the same technology and general principles as other car plants throughout the world. However, it has consistently achieved better results, even when transferred from Japan to Georgetown, Kentucky. One main reason for this is that the workers are engaged in the design and improvement of the system on a continuous basis. Also, each managing director sees as his primary purpose the bequest to his successor of a system of greater capability than that which he inherited. And this 'greater capability' is not quantified in any single measure; it is an aggregate of many measures that most managing directors of car plants would wish for. The key to the success of the TPS, according to the authors' analysis, is attention to detail and an attitude that sustainable improvement can be achieved only over a long period by incremental progress. This approach conflicts directly with the requirements of politicians who make promises to 'cut crime by X per cent in the next three years' or to 'reduce waiting lists by next year'.

There are three further characteristics of complex adaptive systems that I want to use in discussing their implications for policy making. They are important, so please bear with me as I dig a little deeper into the rich field of systems ideas. These characteristics are tensions that all complex adaptive systems balance in one way or another. The three tensions are:

1. adaptability (or flexibility) versus adaptation (or efficiency)
2. change and innovation versus stability
3. centralised control versus decentralisation and autonomy.

Unintended consequences, No 4:

How measures of performance can reduce general system performance

In order to provide the public with an indication of the performance of their local hospitals and also to induce hospital trusts to perform better, the government introduced a star scheme for ranking hospitals. One of the results of this scheme has been to reduce the level of cooperation between hospitals, in some cases to the detriment of patient care.

For example, prior to the ranking scheme, a group of hospitals in the same area might have agreed to pool their A&E resources so as to reduce the admission times – so-called trolley waits – of emergency cases. But now, if one of the hospitals in the group has a zero-star rating because of excessive trolley waits, the other hospitals in the group will be less inclined to share resources with it. They know that their own systems will be stretched by patient transfers from the zero-star hospital. This wariness will be even more acute if one or more of the other hospitals in the group is itself close to a lower ranking owing to trolley waits. Thus rating individual hospitals reduces their incentives to cooperate in improving their collective performance.

As one observer has commented, this is an example of a 'toxic incentive', as 'The sort of altruistic behaviours that are required to support a system-wide approach to patient pathway modernisation are not encouraged by the organisationally focused star systems.'

In general, systems that are fixed at one extreme of any of these tensions will be more vulnerable than those that have a responsive balance. There are also other tensions, such as that between diversity and uniformity, but these are generally controlled by a combination of the three tensions listed above. Thus diversity is consistent with flexibility, innovation and autonomy, whereas uniformity tends to be associated with efficiency, stability and centralised control. These are characteristic differences between, for example, market economies and planned economies.

In many ways the most acute tension, particularly for human-activity systems, is that between flexibility and efficiency. In natural systems, species that are highly adapted exploit niches very effectively, but modest environmental changes can be severely threatening. In contrast, species that are very adaptable can survive in a wide range of environments, but they do not exploit any one environment particularly efficiently. Much the same observations can be made about firms in an economy. In terms of public policy the conflict boils down to the degree to which economic efficiency is pursued.

One example of this tension occurs in the infrastructure used to distribute fuel to end-users. When the gas and electricity industries were publicly owned, these distribution systems erred on the side of flexibility and generally had more capacity than was needed. Since privatisation the emphasis has been on economic efficiency, with a consequent reduction in investment, so that now there are concerns as to whether there is sufficient capacity, especially for future developments.[25] The petrol crisis in September 2000 illustrated a similar general problem. Another good example is '"just in time" inventory systems, which increase efficiency by reducing inventory buffers, but which also mean that a strike in a single plant can rapidly close a whole network of plants'.[26] The pursuit of economic efficiency has, in recent years, tended to override prudent consideration of the robustness of the systems involved, indicating that there is scope for improving the balance of this tension.

Natural systems show the greatest rate of change and adaptation when they are subject to most environmental pressure and less stable. This also tends to be the case for human-activity systems. For example, technologies tend to undergo faster rates of change when they are challenged by a new technology, especially one that threatens to replace them. Our culture values change for a variety of reasons, including novelty, improvements in efficiency and benefits and because it is associated with economic growth and all the benefits that brings. However, the rate of change has now reached a point where it alienates people. The skills an individual learned as a young adult are out of date within a decade and will change several more times before the end of the person's working life. The issues associated with this lack of stability were analysed by Schön[27] 30 years ago, and his analysis and conclusions remain highly relevant. He argues that in our private and public lives we presume that the disruption and change currently causing distress will settle down at some point in the future but also that in practice this stable state never appears. His general conclusions are:

> The loss of the stable state means that our society and all of its institutions are in *continuing* processes of transformation. We cannot expect new stable states that will endure even for our own lifetimes.
>
> We must learn to understand, guide, influence and manage these transformations. We must make the capacity for undertaking them integral to ourselves and our institutions.
>
> We must, in other words, become adept at learning. We must become able not only to transform our institutions, in response to changing situations and requirements; we must invent and develop institutions which are 'learning systems', that is to say, systems capable of bringing about their own continuing transformation.
>
> The task which the loss of the stable state makes imperative, for the person, for our institutions, for our society as a whole, is to learn about learning.

Further aspects of Schön's analysis will be referenced when I discuss alternative strategies for managing entities that have the characteristics of complex adaptive systems.

Much more could be said about complexity and complex adaptive systems. A recent set of articles has reviewed the application of these principles to management,[28] and other authors have applied them health care[29] As the latter group of authors comment, 'The experience of escalating complexity on a practical and personal level can lead to frustration and disillusionment. This may be because there is genuine cause for alarm, but it may simply be that the traditional ways of "getting our heads round the problem" are no longer appropriate.' Echoing the earlier comparison between systems thinking and reductionist thinking the same authors conclude that

> Our learnt instinct with such issues, based on reductionist thinking, is to troubleshoot and fix things – in essence to break down the ambiguity, resolve any paradox, achieve more certainty and agreement, and move into the simple system zone. But complexity science suggests that it is often better to try multiple approaches and let direction arise by gradually shifting time and attention towards those things that seem to be working best.[30]

They cite Schön's reflective practitioner,[31] Kolb's experiential learning model,[32] and the plan–do–study–act cycle of quality improvement as examples of activities that explore new possibilities through experimentation, autonomy and working at the edge of knowledge and experience.

7. Application to Policy

I appreciate that a large number of new and possibly strange concepts and perspectives have been introduced very quickly and with a minimum of explanation and evidence. But it has been essential to cover this core set of ideas in order to illustrate the ways in which systems thinking can inform the policy making process. Even so, I can already hear many of my academic colleagues complaining that I have omitted important ideas, such as Vickers's appreciative systems, the coevolution of a system and its environment, Beer's viable systems, the importance of variety and its management and so on. However, I now wish to develop the arguments about how a systems perspective can contribute to the practical and theoretical issues associated with the making and implementation of policy. I shall start by briefly summarising the systems perspective and then shall list the ways in which, from this perspective, the current approach to policy making and implementation can be *expected to fail*. To the extent that these modes of failure can be recognised by those involved in policy, the systemic perspective will gain credibility. It is one thing to point out what is going wrong but a far more difficult venture to suggest realistic ways of improvement. Being bold I shall propose various strategies that, from the systems perspective, should improve the effectiveness of both the design and implementation of policy. All these strategies involve significant changes in the goals and approach of government, civil servants and those responsible for implementation. Finally, I shall discuss the soft systems method and explain how it could facilitate the changes required.

The systems perspective I have presented challenges the accepted ways of thinking about the world, in particular the ruling paradigms of management and government. A particular set of ideas based on a positivist philosophy, a reductionist way of thinking and a scientific approach have been remarkably successful in increasing our understanding of the inanimate world and our ability to control it. When human-activity systems were relatively simple the same approach succeeded in that area, and borrowed from science and technology for credibility. In the area of natural systems this approach has been both questioned and perceived as failing for some time. Now the frequency of failure in human affairs is also increasing. The core reason for this failure, so the systems practitioners argue, is that the assumptions of separability, linearity, simple causation and predictability are no longer valid. Natural systems have always been, and human systems are becoming, sufficiently complex to make detailed predictions impossible. Complexity is increasing geometrically as advances in communication technologies lower the barriers to interaction. In the terms of a previous metaphor, organisations are taking on more characteristics of birds and losing their stone-like predictability. Under these conditions it is essential that those responsible for managing and governing take on a wider, more holistic perspective, one that includes complexity, uncertainty and ambiguity. Of course a great deal of an individual's way of thinking and assumptions about the world are tacit, ie unconscious and usually unquestioned. It is never easy to make any sort of change in one's way of thinking. One advantage of systems thinking here is that it incorporates a way of thinking about thinking – it helps to make implicit models explicit.

I was involved in teaching systems ideas to adult students for 20 years, and observed that in most cases individuals would become sufficiently open to a new way of thinking only when they became convinced that their previous approach had not, and would not, succeed. From a systems perspective this is predictable, as individuals have evolved a mode of thinking that enables them to cope and adapt to the world as they experience it. It would be inappropriate to abandon a successful mode of thinking without strong evidence that it was inadequate and that a new mode offers tangible improvement. One of the important aspects of systems thinking is that it does not reject or deny the previous modes of thinking. Instead, it *adds* another level of thinking. This is achieved by the strategy of going up a level of abstraction and providing a wider context for thinking processes that normally involve going down levels.

From a systems perspective how would management and policy making fail if the entities being managed were managed as if they were linear, mechanical systems but displayed the characteristics of complex adaptive systems? Most of the modes of failure have already been described; they are summarised here.

- The frequency of unintended consequences would increase. The linear assumptions made when predicting the effects of interventions would not be valid. The managers and policy makers would be surprised, and probably embarrassed, at some outcomes of their interventions.
- Delivery targets would not be met. From a systems perspective this is because the targets would have been established without an appreciation of the capacity of the system involved. For the manager or policy maker it would appear that those responsible for implementation were frustrating his or her goals.
- The main agents within the system would experience greater and greater interference with their daily activities. They would experience this as 'stopping them from getting on with the job'. From a systems perspective this is because the operation of the system is being distorted, and its capacity reduced, by the imposition of one or more quantitative targets that have to be met. As the number of targets increases, there will be an increasing administrative overhead that the delivery professionals will regard as a hindrance and waste of time. They will become progressively more convinced that 'those at the top are becoming more and more out of touch', while those at the top will become more convinced that 'those professionals will just not change'.
- The enterprise being managed would become more fragile and require more frequent interventions in order to cope with events and the unintended consequences of previous interventions. From a systems perspective this is an indication that the capacity of the system is decreasing and that its established modes of adaptation are being eroded.

- The level of acrimony and blame between senior managers and those involved with implementation would increase. This is a predictable consequence of failure to accommodate different perspectives in the formulation of policies. Replacing either the senior people or those responsible for implementation will not improve the situation (because the individuals are not to blame).

I believe that all these dimensions of system failure are observable, in varying degrees, across a range of core government activities.

As well as these general modes of failure, systems thinking predicts that there will be a growing sense of distance, disillusion and frustration in those designing policy, those responsible for implementation and those receiving the service. There are two reasons for this: first, the command-and-control assumptions built into the existing framework and, second, the fact that policy designers cannot, without great effort and a change of approach, appreciate the local context of both what clients need and how this can be achieved. It is ridiculous to imagine that ministers or permanent secretaries should engage with this level of detail, yet some of the targets and directives they issue presume such knowledge. The control-and-command assumptions have two consequences. As pointed out earlier, those further down the hierarchy are treated instrumentally and experience a lack of choice and freedom, to which they instinctively object. More significantly, the implementers will be 'looking the wrong way'. They will be focused on meeting the latest target or directive passed down from above instead of focused on the actual needs of their clientele. Regardless of how the disagreements, blame and disillusion between policy designers and implementing agents resolves itself, the real losers are the public – those the enterprises are supposed to be serving.

Simply adopting systems thinking will not make these difficulties and modes of failure disappear. Systems does not offer a 'silver bullet' that will enable policy makers miraculously to achieve intended outcomes. Rather, adopting a systems approach will require a radical reappraisal of *what* can be achieved as well as the means whereby it might be achieved. If the entities being managed are more like complex adaptive systems than machines, then it might be more appropriate to prioritise the *process of improvement* than a specific goal or target. From this perspective the manager is acknowledging that she or he does not know the degree to which the capacity of the system can be increased but wishes to find out by implementing a process of improvement. Within this general approach several variants are possible.

People who become enthusiastic about systems thinking tend to overstate the relevance of natural systems to the management of human-activity systems. Nevertheless, natural systems do provide a useful source of comparison and metaphor, and suggest an evolutionary strategy for improving systems. This involves encouraging diversity and experimentation and subsequently *discovering* what leads to the best combination of desirable and robust improvement. In his book *Beyond the Stable State*, Schön[33] describes the implementation in the 1960s of a US regional medical programme that ended up using a natural systems model. He points out that the key problems in the original scheme were resolved by devolving not just the design of changes but, more importantly, the evaluation of performance to the regions, where differences in context, experience and opportunities required different approaches. The role of the centre became that of enunciating themes of policy, such as transforming the medical care system and equity of access to care, and subsequently communicating learning from one region to another.

For a management or government wedded to the scientific management approach, an evolutionary strategy raises several difficulties, particularly the inevitable variability of performance and the (apparent) loss of control involved in allowing others to specify the targets and means of evaluation. There are robust ways of addressing these issues, but first a commitment to this strategy is required. With that commitment in place, it can be argued, as I have done, that controlling complex adaptive systems by imposing fixed targets has never been possible. What is more, the requirement of the local agency to demonstrate improvement *in its own terms* is likely to generate a great deal more enthusiasm and commitment to change and success. Uniformity, although much preferred by bureaucrats, can often amount to levelling down rather than up. If there are significant differences among regions, both in terms of context and in the needs of those served, uniformity is not necessarily desirable. Encouraging the process of improvement through diversity *and* communicating the results across the different regions will increase the general rate of improvement. But variations will not disappear. Variation will be part of the engine of continuous improvement.

One of the difficulties that policy makers and senior managers face is that although they may be willing to grant a level of autonomy to well-performing units they will usually strongly resist the idea of extending autonomy to 'problem' units, those that for whatever reason are at the bottom of the league table and a constant source of difficulty. And, so the argument goes, if you cannot grant autonomy to them all then you cannot grant it to any, in order to avoid appearing discriminatory. This is a significant difficulty in public policy making, less so in commercial enterprises. One approach that could resolve the issue is to make use of 'earned autonomy', which is already being explored in some sectors. The idea is that units have to demonstrate certain standards of performance before they are granted an increase in autonomy. This enables policy makers and managers to stay within their own tolerances of risk taking and yet provide additional incentives to poorly performing units to perform better. It also facilitates a manageable level of experimentation. Trials need to be carried out on modest samples so as to minimise the effects of failures, and the 'earned autonomy' approach can be used to accomplish this. It is thus useful in overcoming some of the barriers to adopting an evolutionary or learning approach to policy, but, as explained in detail later, it needs to be combined with deliberate experimentation and evaluation by end-users in order to be effective.

As Schön points out, the diversity approach is one strategy for developing learning within the system. Another strategy for learning is exemplified by the Toyota production system. In this case the learning is applied uniformly and proceeds incrementally. In the TPS any operative can halt the production system by using the 'andon cord', which signals that he or she has identified a problem or abnormality. For a supervisor of a conventional production line this sounds like a nightmare, but it is one of the ways in which the TPS involves the entire workforce in its improvement. In most cases the problem identified can be cleared up quickly enough for production to continue uninterrupted, but where an interruption is necessary the line is stopped. This strategy ensures that any malfunction is corrected as quickly as possible, with the result that the system is maintained close to its maximum capacity. There are many other features of the TPS that contribute to its remarkable success, but they are all embedded in the notion that the steady improvement of the system is the most important priority. What is more, Toyota has demonstrated that these principles, although originating in Japan, work equally well in plants in Europe and America. The improvement being sought, and achieved, is not specified by a single target. The improvement in output must not jeopardise quality or customer satisfaction or worker turnover rate or profitability or the continuous improvement of the system and its products. The TPS practices help to create and foster feedback mechanisms that ensure learning. One side effect of this is that the TPS does not use the normal array of computerised information systems that are used elsewhere for targeting and monitoring. The entire system is customer-driven: cars are made only when they have been ordered.

The TPS is one specific example of a learning organisation. There are many other examples, and a rich literature[34] is available for managers wishing to pursue the learning organisation approach. The key characteristics that distinguish a learning organisation are its attitude towards failure and the decision-making processes. Note that within the TPS a worker who stops a production line by noticing a problem or abnormality does so knowing that there is no blame or recrimination involved – it is simply the best way to ensure that the production line operates correctly. Another good example of tolerance of failure arose when the Eden project in Cornwall opened. The managing director Tim Smit called the staff together and said, 'Tomorrow, people will ask you for things, or to do things, we haven't thought of. If you respond in a way which goes wrong, no one will blame you. If you do nothing, I'll sack you.'[35]

Failure is something that management and governments tend to shy away from. They have difficulty owning up to failures, and rather than learn in detail they will simply 'not do anything like that again!' This is a difficulty with *all* learning approaches to management or policy, because there will inevitably be failures. But in the context of a learning culture or learning organisation failures are simply opportunities to learn, not occasions for blame, recrimination and point-scoring. *While failure is unacceptable, learning is not possible – with the paradoxical result that failures will continue.* Of all the changes required to engage fully with a systems approach, this is probably the most important one, and the one likely to be the greatest obstacle.

As the issue of attitude towards failure is central, I want to discuss it further. In organisations that are averse to owning up to and learning from failure, there will exist some sort of blame culture, and it will inhibit telling the truth. This is colloquially known as 'arse covering'; it operates in plague proportions in the civil service. There are sound reasons for this, based on the way that civil servants are rarely praised in public but may be censured by parliamentary committees. Sir Derek Raynor, a senior civil servant in the Heath and Thatcher governments, considered failure avoidance as *the* dominant trait of the Whitehall culture. In his evidence to the Expenditure Committee,[36] he stated:

> Efficiency in the Civil Service is dependent, as in business, on motivation, and whereas in business one is judged by overall success, in my experience the civil servant tends to be judged by failure. This inevitably conditions his approach to his work in dealing with the elimination of unnecessary paper work, and in eliminating unnecessary monitoring, and leads to the creation of an unnecessary number of large committees, all of which leads to delays in decision making and the blurring of responsibility.

The inevitable result is that information is distorted at every level because no one wishes to communicate 'bad news' or to expose themselves to blame.

Let me recapitulate my argument. I outlined the way in which a systems perspective challenges a deep-seated set of assumptions concerning how to think about and manage the world. I then set out the types of failure that a systems practitioner would expect if a complex adaptive system were being managed under the traditional, non-systemic assumptions. These modes of failure are recognisably part of the current difficulties experienced by government in trying to improve a wide range of public services. Although systems thinking cannot provide a magic solution to these failures, it can suggest different approaches, based on processes rather than goals, that provide the best possible means of avoiding the failures. All the approaches that satisfy these requirements are based on the idea of *learning*. I have also started to discuss some of the obstacles that will need to be overcome and pointed to other benefits of tackling these obstacles, particularly more truthful communication.

This general argument would have the support of most, if not all, of the systems community. There may be disagreement about the relative importance of aspects of the argument that I have laboured and of others that I have overlooked or dealt with cursorily. But the overall conclusion, that managing enterprises that display the characteristics of complex adaptive systems requires learning, is robust. In short, systems practice in this area must be based on creating effective learning. There are also differences between practitioners about how to generate that learning. However, one method, soft systems methodology, stands out as being very successful in this regard.

8. Soft Systems Methodology

Soft systems methodology is a structured way to establish a *learning system* for investigating messy problems. The process has been succinctly summarised as follows:

> SSM is a methodology that aims to bring about improvement in areas of social concern by activating in the people involved in the situation a learning cycle which is ideally never ending. The learning takes place through the iterative process of using systems concepts to reflect upon and debate perceptions of the real world, taking action in the real world, and again reflecting on the happenings using systems concepts. The reflection and debate is structured by a number of systemic models. These are conceived of as holistic ideal types of certain aspects of the problem situation rather than accounts of it. It is taken as given that no objective and complete account of a problem situation can be provided.[37]

SSM has been used widely for the past 30 years; there are many descriptions of its application to both commercial and public policy.[38]

The general sequence of an SSM enquiry is illustrated in Figure 3. This represents SSM's original form. It has been refined and extended over the years, and reflects the ways in which practitioners have found it useful to adapt the process to specific contexts. A more comprehensive version of the methodology is now available.[39] For my purposes, however, the simpler representation shown here is adequate.

Once a problem has been identified, the participants in the SSM process represent their perspective on and involvement with the problem by using one or more rich pictures (as shown in Figure 2). From the rich pictures and the associated exploration of the context, a number of themes may be identified; these can be issue-based or primary-task themes. Descriptions of these themes, called 'root definitions', are developed, and then are modelled as if they were a system. This is the stage at which the method goes up a level of abstraction and loses detail while maintaining the essential connectedness. Applying the relevant system is not an attempt to identify a 'real' system in the external world; it is a construct used to clarify thinking about certain aspects of the problem. Root definitions usually start with the words 'A system to . . .', and it is always recognised that this description is made from a particular perspective. The choice of theme and root definition is a matter of choice. With experience, those that are most likely to lead to learning and insight are chosen.

Figure 3.
The seven-step process of SSM

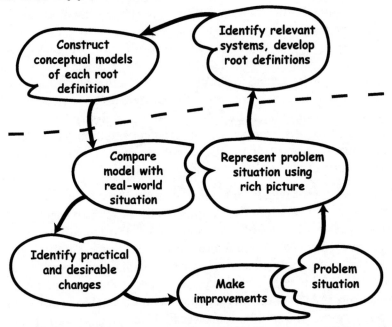

A root definition is a formal way of specifying the purpose of the system of interest and its intended core transformation. This definition is then used to construct a 'conceptual model' of the sequence of activities that would be required to accomplish the purpose. The model consists of a modest number of verbs linked in sequence; it is not quantitative or computerised. This idealised sequence of activities can now be compared with those that actually occur in the real world, and differences or omissions can be identified. This comparison marks the return from the higher level of abstraction to the level of the real world, which are shown separated by the dashed line in Figure 3. The comparison can be used to generate an agenda for improvement. If the participants are in a position to implement some or all of the changes, then the sequence can be repeated. The extended version of SSM adds explicit analyses of the culture of the organisation, including its 'political system'.

My own and others' experience of using SSM suggests that its main strength is its ability to bring to the surface different perceptions of the problem and structure these in a way that all involved find fruitful. Because the process is strange to most participants, it also fosters greater openness and self-awareness. The process is very effective at team-building and joint problem-solving. It is extremely difficult to capture the essence of participating in an SSM exercise because it is the experience itself that is powerful, meaningful and rewarding.

SSM is not universally applicable. One observer has commented:

> SSM is likely to be acceptable where operational staff in the problem situation are viewed as 'stakeholders' and stakeholder ownership of improvements seen as an essential prerequisite for change. This view supports the implicit premise of SSM that action learning and organisational development are parallel and interconnected processes.[40]

This point reinforces those made earlier regarding the participation of those implementing or affected by a policy; without their participation the learning will be incomplete and inadequate.

9. Obstacles to Learning

I have argued that in the face of complexity learning is central to systems practice in management. I have also described one approach based on the creation of learning systems. However, within government, ie the political system and the civil service, there is a significant array of obstacles to learning that need to be addressed if any form of systems practice is to occur, let alone produce more effective policies.

The two most important obstacles, namely fear of failure and avoidance of diversity or variety, have already been discussed, and suggestions have been made as to how they might be circumvented. In practice, embarking on policies that would inevitably lead to some failures and significant variations in the standard of public service is likely to be regarded as naïve and close to political suicide. The reasons for this are the adversarial political system and a bipartisan press. Acknowledgement of a 'failure' would be used by opposition politicians and media as a basis for attack and denigration. When politicians are in opposition they are not interested in the effectiveness of policy processes; they are focused on scoring enough points, in the eyes of the electorate, to win the next election. It is only when those politicians come into office and try to carry out their own reforms that they confront the ineffectiveness of the 'machinery of government'. In order for 'failures' to be politically acceptable, it would be essential to win the argument that experimentation and discovery are a more effective route to improving system performance than centralised design.

At one level this argument has already been won, as there is now widespread agreement that markets are more effective and efficient than planned economies. Markets succeed precisely because they foster variety, diversity and innovation and evolve under the pressure of selection. Clearly, markets also give rise to 'failures', companies that never make it or succeed for a while and then fail. But the only selection criterion operating in markets is greed; companies do not ultimately succeed by providing public services, fostering racial equality, reducing poverty or enhancing the education of disabled people. Companies succeed by making money, and the rigours of the market insist that this be so. Although markets provide a paradigmatic example of how variety, innovation, selection and failure can operate, they are not perceived as providing an exemplar that can readily be followed in public policy. What is needed is an evolutionary system where the pressure of selection on service-providers matches all the values and requirements of the clientele, not just pecuniary assessment of worth. League tables are an attempt to generate that pressure, but, as argued earlier, they distort the system by using simplistic measures of performance. If public policy were based on fostering innovation and diversity, then it would be an appropriate function of central government to act as the selection agent, representing as it does the democratic balance of values within the electorate. Thus, rather than imposing a multiplicity of universal targets on all schools, hospitals and police forces, the role of the centre shifts to evaluating and selecting the variants that best fulfil the perceived needs of the public in a particular area.

This change of role raises another obstacle to learning, namely the commitment to a command-and-control style of government. Senior politicians and civil servants have in common strong ambitions and characters that seek and enjoy power. There is thus a tacit agreement that the centralised exercise of power is the right and proper function of those in charge of government. When I discussed this pamphlet with colleagues, one remarked that, although 'some ministers and civil servants know that command and control is not the way to go, the individuals still fall for it.' It has also been suggested that the success of the reformers in the Labour Party in the 1990s, where a small group effectively transformed the party, has conditioned the New Labour government to a command and control approach.[41] There is no doubt that New Labour has succeeded in presenting itself as a more coherent government through tight central control of policy and public relations. But the success in party reform and public relations is not necessarily well suited to the development and implementation of effective policy.

One of the key reasons why the command-and-control style fails with the current system of governance is that many of the agencies responsible for delivering essential public services are not directly answerable to ministers. This means that it is actually impossible to force a command down to the front line. (The military language is used by people attempting to manage the system!) Instead, the command system has to rely on incentives, targets and flows of information that become distorted through the multiple perspectives of those receiving the communications. This drives the argument back into the area of complexity, uncertainty and so on, which were used earlier in advocacy of a different approach to policy, based on systems thinking.

Many of the obstacles to learning that have been identified would be corrected if there were an effective feedback loop linking policy design to outcomes. If ministers and civil servants were regularly aware that their hard-won policies and budgets did not yield the outcomes they desired, then a learning process would be started. There are several reasons why this feedback does not occur, but by far the most important one is a lack of time. The pressures of work and new contexts demand that today's issues are tackled without the wisdom that might be gleaned from the past. But time pressure is itself part of a positive feedback loop that promises a deteriorating future, both for the health of these managers and civil servants and the organisations for which they are responsible. The positive feedback loop is illustrated in Figure 4.

Figure 4.
The positive feedback loop of deterioration in policy owing to lack of time

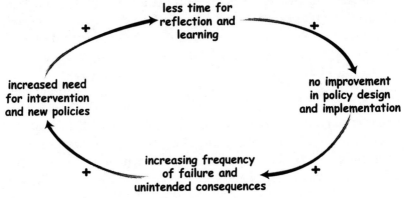

The positive feedback loop currently operates in a harmful way. The same loop could be made to work positively by allowing one policy team sufficient time for reflection and ensuring that this is used to improve the policy design and implementation process. Then the improved policies will lead to a reduction in the number of failures and consequences and in turn to a reduced need for new policies and interventions. It is unrealistic for a whole department or policy area to break out of the loop at the same time, but it is feasible for this to be done in one domain. To the degree that a breakout is successful in that domain, time is liberated for similar improvements in others. Presuming that with an initial increase in time policy making can be made more effective, the process can bootstrap itself and lead to a significant general improvement. The key is to be able to use the initial effort effectively. The arguments I have put forward suggest that this involves evaluating past performance, reflecting on it and learning how to be more effective – in short, establishing a learning system to improve policy.

The importance of breaking out of the ever diminishing time available for policy creation and implementation has been emphasised from another perspective by Verma.[42] He points out that time pressure forces policy makers to seek the most efficient means of resolving policy issues and that this pursuit of efficiency comes at a cost.

Reductionism works by cultivating the dominance of one or a small set of ideas over all others. It is powerful and efficient. Reducing something to an essential set of properties or attributes allows us to abstract from an otherwise difficult-to-manage set of complicated, interwoven questions. It is an exercise in pruning that makes rigor and efficiency possible ... The cost is in what gets pruned away. Although most managers and planners agree that efficiency is not the only value and that there are other compelling concerns, when it comes to actual practice all else falls under the axe of what is efficient ...

Comprehensiveness is about recognising the importance of preparedness, sharing, trust, loyalty, entrepreneurship, and risk-taking ability in decision-making. These are normative values that demand a theory of ethics, not criteria that can be feasibly optimised within an analytic calculus. .... The problem of comprehensiveness in management and planning is not one of adding more variables or more data. Rather it is about restoring values that are the key to the practices of these professions but that have been systematically excised from them.

Another factor contributing to the lack of effective feedback is the tradition of secrecy. Sir John Hoskyns, former head of Mrs Thatcher's Downing Street Policy Unit, has commented:

> With confidence and competence so much lower than they should be, it is not surprising that Whitehall fiercely defends its tradition of secrecy. The Official Secrets Act and the Thirty Year Rule, by hiding peacetime fiascos, as if they were military disasters, protects ministers and officials from embarrassment. They also ensure that there is no learning curve.[43]

As a measure of protection from embarrassment can assist learning, so a measure of secrecy is not inconsistent with establishing a learning process. But in the recent past, as Sir John notes, secrecy has been used not in the service of learning but in its obstruction.

I was recently involved with a policy project in government, and was pleasantly surprised when one of the early meetings was scheduled to discuss stakeholder involvement. I presumed, foolishly as it turned out, that the stakeholders to be discussed were those likely to be affected by or involved in implementing policy decisions. I was surprised to find that in practice stakeholder analysis pertained to other departments in government. It is true that to a degree they were stakeholders, in the sense used by systems practitioners that they might be affected by policies and involved in implementing them. But in reality the exercise was principally about the individuals and departments that had to be kept informed and happy if a proposal were to be steered through the turf wars and interpersonal politics in government. Although not often addressed, this has become a serious constraint on all areas of policy making. These constraints mean that many policies are not determined by the best interests of the eventual recipients, be they the disabled, the unemployed, students, directors or whoever. The policies are actually determined by what can be squeezed through the Treasury, Number 10 and other dominant Whitehall departments. The long process of negotiation and horse-trading between departments also adds to the time pressures on those responsible for policy.

The demands of this negotiating and horse-trading are one reason why systems thinking is used less in public policy than in business. Interdepartmental battles tend to make the policy process inward-looking. They also reinforce the dominant modes of debate, in this case a positivist philosophy and neo-classical economics. In business, managers at all levels are far more interested in what works, partly because they are judged on actual delivered results but also because they perceive themselves as an integral part of the delivery of whatever goods and services are involved. In contrast, the senior policy makers, both politicians and civil servants, do not perceive themselves as part of the delivery system – and are certainly not judged by what is or is not delivered to the end-users. Whereas most business managers are eager to discover techniques or approaches that might give them a commercial edge, the upper echelons of the policy world are relatively closed to criticism and new ideas. The need to be immersed in the politics of Whitehall accounts for much of this tendency.

I once had the misfortune to be involved in a policy area in which a civil servant bore a personal grudge against someone working in the area but outside government. The grudge constrained and, to a large degree, determined that policy. It was an ugly performance that left everyone involved feeling embarrassed and uncertain how to raise or deal with the issue. I have been told that this is not a particularly unusual occurrence. In retrospect, what was most shocking about it was that, although all those involved knew what was going on, no one was able to challenge it or have it discussed openly. Actual policy decisions were justified on other grounds that were fairly arbitrary, making it difficult to mount a challenge. This is an extreme example of the loss of professional values referred to in the quotation from Verma above. This loss seems to occur at all levels. For example, the acknowledged antipathy between Ken Livingstone and ministers in the current government appears to have distorted the policy process regarding the refurbishment of the London Underground.

It is inevitable that, when an area is examined critically, the result is a preponderance of negatives, things that are wrong or are obstacles to progress. There is insufficient space here to correct this imbalance, but suffice it to say that there is much of great value in the British form of government and the traditions of its civil service. I have been deeply impressed by the commitment to democracy, honesty, impartiality and, despite repeated scandals, the absence of corruption. There are innumerable valuable traditions embedded in the procedures of government and the ethics of the civil service. The problem that I am addressing has been succinctly expressed by Ison: 'Traditions are very important to a culture because they embed what has, over time, been judged to be a useful practice. The risk for any culture is that a tradition can become a blind spot when it evolves into a practice lacking any manner of critical reflection being connected to it.'[44]

The barriers I have identified that prevent critical reflection and learning are:

- A culture that is averse to failure
- A desire for uniformity in public services that stifles innovation and variety
- An adversarial political system, supported by the media, that uses failure as a way of scoring points
- Shared assumptions between politicians and civil servants that command and control is the correct way to exercise power
- A lack of feedback on the results of policies
- A lack of time to do anything other than cope
- A tradition of secrecy that is used to stifle feedback and learning
- A system that requires policies to be negotiated with competing power centres in government
- Turf wars between departments and individuals
- Loss of professional standards under the knife of efficiency.

I have also made suggestions about how some of these barriers might be addressed. However, one of the chief tenets of systems thinking is that it is essential that institutional and organisational change is undertaken by those within; only they appreciate the constraints, and ultimately it is they who have to implement and carry forward the changes. It is impossible that all these barriers can be removed quickly. What is possible is that with a commitment to making change by way of learning, there will be sufficient flexibility to start managing complexity more effectively.

10. Systems Practice

My arguments and examples have, I trust, made it clear that systems thinking can make sense of a great deal of what is confusing, counterintuitive and frustrating in policy making and managing large organisations. However, the benefits of adopting a systems approach are much greater than just a set of ideas that can yield useful insights. My experience of applying systems practice in academic and commercial organisations is that there is a significant improvement in effectiveness as well as understanding. Because systems thinking has not yet been embraced significantly by makers of public policy, it is not possible to be certain that it will yield similar results, but all the indications are that this is indeed the case. In particular, systems thinking overcomes the major deficiencies in the traditional, linear, mechanistic approach to policy, and systems practice provides a viable alternative to the command-and-control approach.

It is impossible to specify precisely the changes that the adoption of systems practice to policy would yield because they will be highly context-dependent. However, there are some generic changes that arise as a result of systems practice, the main ones being:

- Interventions would introduce learning processes rather than specifying outcomes or targets. The key to establishing learning systems is an increased tolerance of failure, continuous feedback on effectiveness and a willingness to foster diversity and innovation.

- The emphasis would be on improving general system effectiveness, as judged by the clients or users of the system. This cannot be accomplished by using simple quantitative measures of perform-ance; it needs to take account of a range of qualitative as well as quantitative features chosen and assessed by the end-users.

- The process of designing, formulating and implementing policies will be based more on facilitation of improvements than on control of the organisation/system. The aim should be to provide a minimum specification that creates an environment in which innovative, complex behaviours can emerge. The key is to provide clear direction, boundaries that must not be crossed, resources and permissions.

- The process of engaging with agents and stakeholders in a policy area will be based more upon listening and co-researching and less upon telling and instructing. This will require the policy process somehow to break out of the Whitehall horse-trading system and engage seriously with implementation agencies, end-users and other stakeholders at the point of delivery affected by proposed changes.

- Implementation will include deliberate strategies for innovation, evaluation, learning and reflection. This would normally involve obtaining feedback about the effects of initial interventions and using this to make modifications as appropriate. A key part of the evaluation and reflection process will involve selection of success-ful approaches and, equally importantly, the demise of those that have not succeeded.

This list has significant similarities to some of the changes that have been identified as necessary in a recent PIU study entitled 'Better Policy Delivery and Design'.[45] According to the document's summary:

Past experience shows that delivery is rarely a one-off task. It is best understood not as a linear process – leading from policy ideas through implementation to a change on the ground – but rather as a more circular process involving continuous learning, adapta-tion and improvement, with policy changing in response to imple-mentation as well as vice versa.

The paper shows that delivery of public services always depends on the actions of people and institutions that cannot be directly controlled by central government, departments and agencies.

Although short-term results can be achieved through direction, in the long run it is more efficient and effective to motivate and empower than to issue detailed commands. In several policy areas government is therefore seeking to define a new balance in which:

- fewer but clearer outcome targets are combined with
- greater freedom for managers to adapt and innovate, alongside
- clearer expectations that poor performance will be tackled decisively.

Similar sentiments have been echoed by Gordon Brown. He has remarked, 'Whatever people said in the past we know Whitehall does not know best, and we know that effective service delivery for families and communities cannot come from command and control, but requires local initiative and accountability.'[46]

Organisations of all sorts and sizes have to change themselves. This was a key conclusion from the discussion of complex adaptive systems, and it is a major conclusion of all systems work. To the degree that an organisation displays adaptive behaviour it will strive to retain its internal culture, processes and values – that is what the adaptation seeks to preserve. Thus an organisation's initial response to all outside pressures and changes in its environment will be to adapt and adjust so as to maintain these core attributes. This theory applies to the entities managed by government, and to the policy making process itself. Just as it is an error for government to adopt a command-and-control and over-prescriptive approach to agencies that execute its policies, so it would be a crass error for this exposition to provide a detailed prescription for change within the policy process.

One of my colleagues suggested that the way to end this pamphlet would be to provide an example of how systems practice might be applied in a specific policy context. This suggestion was attractive, if only because it would enable those involved to see a relevant application of systems ideas, and also to see that the task of change is readily achievable. However, to do this convincingly requires more detailed knowledge of a policy area than I possess. Also, it would in effect prescribe a solution when what is needed is the creation of a learning system. One of the greatest difficulties faced by people using SSM for the first time is that part-way through the process their thinking has shifted

Unintended consequences, No 5:
The dangers of injecting money into a system without engaging the participants

Increasing the funding to the health system may not have the desired consequences. Here are three examples of ways in which additional funds have had unintended consequences – and have not led to significant improvements in the care of patients.

It has long been recognised that junior doctors in hospitals are often asked to work unreasonably long hours. In order to provide hospital trusts with an incentive to tackle this problem and reduce the occurrence of excessively long hours, the government introduced a system of additional payments to junior doctors. These payments were made in proportion to the intensity of work undertaken by the junior doctors. The scheme ended up costing more than twice as much as expected, because the people who really had an incentive were the junior doctors. As a result of the scheme they kept meticulous records of hours worked, and received greater compensation.

The decision to allocate funds that could be spent in the private sector so as to reduce waiting times completely undermined the negotiations with consultants to undertake more operations in the NHS. The negotiations were intended to gain the consultants' agreement to undertake additional cases at a reduced rate. However, they realised that all they had to do was wait and the new money would become available to them through the private route.

Increasing the funds available for health care has actually raised some NHS costs. The reason for this is that as health care funding has increased, so spending by some local governments on social care has declined. The result is that the NHS either has to make up the shortfall in social care funding or find its beds filled with people who need social care rather than medical assistance.

enough for them to 'see a solution' – and these 'solutions' become an obstacle to further learning. Systems practice does involve generating new insights, new approaches, new procedures and so on, but it is critical to the overall enterprise that they emerge from a learning process in which as many stakeholders, end-users and delivery agents are involved as possible. It is only by integrating their different perspectives and values into the learning process that the resulting actions will deal effectively with inherent complexity, including multiplicity of views and aspirations.

What can actually be done to engage with systems practice in a policy context? Clearly, it is right and proper for ministers to determine *what* should be the priorities and directions of government policy and action. The error made in the command-and-control style is that the minister, or other high-level officials, also attempts to prescribe *how* policies should be implemented. It is the over-prescriptive nature of policy that inhibits innovation, learning and paying attention to the needs of those being served. Maintaining a distinction between the *what* and the *how* of policy has proved to be useful for opening a space within which new approaches can be explored.

Ideally, once the *what* has been established, an SSM exercise, involving as many stakeholders, delivery agencies and end-users as feasible, should be used to establish an agenda for action. The basic reason for suggesting SSM is that it provides

a methodology that aims to bring about improvement in areas of social concern by activating in the people involved in the situation a learning cycle which is ideally never-ending. The learning takes place through the iterative process of using systems concepts to reflect upon and debate perceptions of the real world, taking action in the real world, and again reflecting on the happenings using systems concepts.[47]

However, any other process that achieves the same learning cycle would serve.

The policy output from the process should be as unprescriptive about means as possible. Ideally, it should be a minimum specification, which

- **establishes the direction** of the change required clearly
- **sets boundaries** that may not be crossed by any implementation strategy
- **allocates resources**, but without specifying how they must be deployed. The granting of resources should be for a sufficiently long period of time that a novel approach can be explored thoroughly (one year is normally inadequate), but it should not be

open-ended. It should be made clear what additional resources will be granted if the approach is successful and what the timescale for withdrawal of resources will be if it is not successful

- **grants permissions**, ie explicitly specifies the areas of discretion in which local agencies or managers can exercise innovation and choice
- **specifies core evaluation requirements**, for example frequency of output but leaves the detailed design to local agencies. Part of the core specification will be a requirement that end-users have accessible and relevant means for providing their feedback and evaluations.

Whatever the policy it will need to be revisited periodically to continue the learning cycle. In the light of feedback, decisions need to be taken about future resource allocations, the degree of success of different approaches and the revision of the policy guidance. This may involve modification to all or parts of the minimum specification. There should also be in place an effective communication system among the different agencies implementing the policy so that what is learned (about what is working and what is not) can be disseminated and adapted to local conditions.

This is not entirely idealistic. There is a growing awareness that changes along these lines are necessary, as evidenced by the quotations from government reviews and officials throughout this work. What has been missing up to now is a coherent theoretical framework within which the various initiatives for change can be seen more holistically and developed coherently. There are a number of initiatives and opportunities that are already moving in the direction proposed here. Examples include the experiment with cannabis possession in Brixton and the use of earned autonomy in high-performing schools and hospitals.

Ultimately, whether a process of change takes place depends upon the willingness of those in the government and civil service, particularly the senior policy makers and advisers – just as effective changes in any organisation depend upon the learning abilities of those within the organisation. The challenge, as always, is to be open to other perspectives and to be open to learning. This in its turn depends upon the intellectual and emotional awareness of the individuals involved. Many people have had the experience of making an initial appraisal of someone and having this challenged by learning more about the person's circumstances or background. When the initial appraisal changes, there is a significant difference in the emotional response to that person and in the way they are perceived and their actions interpreted. Similar shifts of perception and emotional engagement are common in systems work, and are an essential component in breaking out of the mental traps that confine us. In the case of those making public policy, the stakes are higher and the potential benefits that much greater. Sir Andrew Turnbull, the incoming Cabinet Secretary, has already indicated his openness to trying out new ways of thinking and finding new combinations of insider and outsider expertise in the policy making process.[48] There is an increasingly open debate about the need for the senior civil service to reform and reinvent itself in order to provide the kind of guidance and governance that the wider British public service needs in order to thrive.[49]

The challenge now is not suddenly to attempt to institute a new and rigid mode of analysis in every aspect of public policy making. It is to draw together the opportunities for developing and scaling up the impact of systems approaches and to offer the experience of system improvement through systems thinking to as many public servants as possible. This could be done in various ways:

- choosing a number of priority areas and focusing on the development of new methods in them; there are, inevitably, many candidates.
- individual government departments and public agencies could begin to experiment with their own approach, through the multiplicity of strategy and innovation units now being created and through engagement with outside partners.
- developing a capacity for systems analysis and collaboration across sectors, at the local and regional level, and making it a clear priority.
- re-examining the career paths and training opportunities of the mass of civil and public servants and reviewing the role of leadership and management training.
- accelerating the development of approaches that seek to generate service-level innovation from within mainstream practice by everyday practitioners – teachers, doctors and police officers, for example – rather than treating piloting and innovation as separate and specalised activities.

- focusing attention on the tools and strategies available for accelerating the spread of innovation and learning *across* complex public service organisations, rather than waiting for good innovation to spread to the top and then be rebroadcast back out.

This kind of approach should also help to clarify a note of warning for those strategic units that have been set up at the heart of government to encourage a long-term approach and coordinated strategy. There is a clear need for coordination. But in the long run a strategy that seeks to achieve better implementation simply by rewriting the policy of other departments and agencies and relying on command-and-control powers to do so will be unable to achieve the kinds of improvements in the whole system's capacity that a more holistic approach clearly demands.

Health is the area of policy where the opportunity and the challenge are greatest, and the British government has now made an irrevocable commitment to increasing the priority and resourcing of health care. To achieve a comparable improvement in system performance, the government will have to rely on a wider repertoire of implementation and learning approaches than it currently has at its disposal.

The ultimate goal is the creation of a system of government that can *learn for itself*, on a continuous basis, and be guided by democratically legitimated goals and priorities. Earlier I commented that when I taught systems thinking to students they resisted its adoption until they were confronted by the clear failure of their existing thinking – and that this was a rational behaviour that is predictable using systems ideas of adaptation and survival. This observation is echoed in Kuhn's analysis of scientific revolutions,[50] in which he quotes Max Planck that 'a new scientific truth does not triumph by convincing its opponents and making them see the light, but rather because its opponents eventually die, and a new generation grows up that is familiar with it.'[51] It would, in my view, be a disaster if public policy has to fail catastrophically before systems ideas are taken up. And it would not be much better if we have to wait 30 years for the current generation of senior civil servants and politicians to die off.

References

1 See, for example, AO Hirschman and CE Lindblom, 'Lindblom on Policy Making', *Behavioural Science* 7 (1962). For alternatives to the rational strategy, see, for example, HA Simon, *The new Science of Management Decision* (Harper & Row 1960) and JG March, 'Theories of Choice and Making Decisions', *Society* 20, no 1 (1982).

2 See the two-part in-depth analysis by Nick Davies in *Guardian*, 14 June 2001, pp 20–1 and 15 June 2001, pp 18–19.

3 R Axelrod and MD Cohen, *Harnessing Complexity: Organizational implications of a scientific frontier* (New York: The Free Press, Simon & Schuster, 1999).

4 See reference 3, p.26

5 A Seldon, 'The Net Blair Effect: A foundation government' in A Seldon (ed), *The Blair Effect* (London: Little Brown and Company, 2001).

6 'Professional Policy Making for the Twenty First Century', report by Strategic Policy Making Team, Cabinet Office, September 1999.

7 Tom Bentley, 'Letting go: complexity, individualism and the left', *Renewal*, 10, no1 (Winter 2002).

8 G Mulgan, 'Systems thinking and the practice of government', paper presented to OU Conference on Managing Complexity, May 2001, published in *Systemist*, 23 (Nov 2001), pp 22–9.

9 The use of the term 'mess' comes from RL Ackoff, *Redesigning the Future* (1974). It has been exemplified and expanded in C Eden, S Jones and D Sims, *Messing about with Problems* (Oxford: Pergamon Press, 1983).

10 P Checkland,'Systems' in *International Encyclopaedia of Business and Management* (Thomson Business Press, 1997).

11 L von Bertalanffy, *General Systems Theory* (Cambridge MA: MIT Press, 1968).

12 See, for example, S Beer, *The Heart of the Enterprise* (Wiley, 1979) or S Beer, *Designing Freedom* (Wiley, 1974).

13 P Checkland, *Systems Thinking, Systems Practice* (Wiley, 1981). See also P Checkland and J Scholes, *Soft Systems Methodology in Action* (Wiley, 1990).

14 DA Schön and M Rein, *Frame Reflection* (Basic Books, 1994).

15 G Vickers, *Freedom in a Rocking Boat* (Penguin, 1972).

16 DH Meadows, J Randers and WW Behrens, *Limits to Growth* (New York: Universe Books, 1972).

17 P Checkland, op.cit.

18 P Plsek, 'Why won't the NHS do as it's told', plenary address, NHS Conference, July 2001. (See also *Leading Edge* 1 (October 2001), published by the NHS Confederation, London.)

19 See, for example, H Maturana and F Varela, *The Tree of Knowledge* (Boston: Shambala, 1987). For a more accessible account, including the relation of this theory to systems, see F Capra, *The Web of Life* (London: Harper Collins, 1996).

20 S Caulkin, 'On target for destruction', *Observer*, 5 August 2001.

21 FP Brookes, *The mythical man-month* (Addison Wesley, 1975 and 1995).

22 M Horne, *Classroom Assistance* (London: Demos, 2002).

23 HT Johnson and A Broms, *Profit beyond measure* (London: Nicholas Brealey, 2000). The authors link their excellent case study data to a less convincing argument in favour of a new management style, which they refer to as 'management by means'.

24 W Edwards Deming, *Out of the Crisis* (Cambridge MA, 1986).

25 For a fuller discussion, see 'The Energy Review', Performance and Innovation Unit, Cabinet Office, February 2002.

26 From Axelrod and Cohen, *Harnessing Complexity*. Note that in the case of the petrol crisis the 'just in time' delivery system only exacerbated the problem. The capacity of vehicle fuel tanks is such that a spate of panic buying can always exhaust the storage facilities at local fuel stations.

27 DA Schön, *Beyond the Stable State* (London: Temple Smith, 1971).

28 RD Stacey, *Strategic management and organisational dynamics: the challenge of complexity*, 3rd edn (London: Financial Times, 1999).

29 PE Plsek and T Greenhalgh, 'The challenge of complexity in health care', *British Medical Journal (BMJ)* 323 (15 September 2001), p 625; T Wilson and T Holt, 'Complexity and clinical care', *BMJ* 323 (22 September 2001), p 685; PE Plsek and T Wilson, 'Complexity, leadership and management in healthcare organisations', *BMJ* 323 (29 September 2001), p 746; and SW Fraser and T Greenhalgh, 'Coping with complexity: educating for capability', *BMJ* 323 (6 October 2001), p 799.

30 PE Plsek and T Greenhalgh, op.cit.

31 DA Schön, *The reflective practitioner* (New York: Basic Books, 1983).

32 DA Kolb, *Experiential learning: Experience as the source of learning and development* (Englewood Cliffs, NJ: Prentice Hall, 1984).

33 DA Schön, *Beyond the Stable State* (London: Temple Smith, 1971).

34 See, for example, B Garratt, *The learning organisation* (Fontana, 1987); DA Schön and C Argyris, *Organisational Learning: A theory in action perspective* (Addison Wesley, 1978); and P Senge, *The Fifth Dimension: The art and practice of the learning organisation* (1995).

35 T Smit, *Eden* (Bantam Books, 2001).

36 Eleventh Report from the Expenditure Committee, Session 1976–7, 'The Civil Service', Vol. II, Part II, p 659, quoted in P Hennessy, *Whitehall* (Pimlico, 2001).

37 I von Bulow, 'The bounding of a problem situation and the concept of systems boundary in SSM', *Journal of Applied Systems Analysis* 16 (1989), pp 35–41.

38 The authoritative references are given in note 12 above. For a simple step-by-step introduction, see D Patching, *Practical Soft Systems Analysis* (FT Prentice Hall, 1990). For accounts of experience in its use, see note 39 below.

39 Quotation taken from Sheila Challender's contribution in P Checkland et al., 'The emergent properties of SSM in Use: A symposium by reflective practitioners', *Systemic Practice and Action Research* 13, no 6 (2000), p 799.

40 P Checkland, op.cit.

41 For fuller discussion, see Tom Bentley, op.cit.

42 N Verma *'Similarities, Connections and Systems'* (Lexington Books, Maryland, 1998)

43 Quoted in Hennessy, *Whitehall*, p 344.

44 RL Ison and D Russell, *Agricultural Extension and Rural Development: Breaking out of traditions* (Cambridge: Cambridge University Press, 2000).

45 'Better Policy Delivery and Design: A discussion paper', Performance and

Innovation Unit, Cabinet Office, March
2001.
46 G Brown, speech to LGA, 19
December 2001.
47 DA Schön, *Beyond the Stable State.*
48 *The Times*, 1 May 2002.
49 C Leadbeater, *Innovate from within: an
open letter to the new Cabinet Secretary*
(London: Demos, 2002).
50 TS Kuhn, *The structure of scientific revolutions* (University of Chicago Press,
1970).
51 M Planck, *Scientific Autobiography and
Other Papers*, tr F Gaynor (New York,
1949).

Bibliography

Axelrod, R and Cohen, MD, *Harnessing Complexity: Organizational implications of a scientific frontier*. New York: The Free Press, 1999. This book is based firmly in hard-systems thinking, and shows how new ways of thinking about complexity can produce viable strategies for management and product development. The concept of a complex adaptive system presented in this book is different from that developed in this pamphlet, but the general conclusions are similar – namely that the increase in complexity cannot be wished away or ignored and that it will frustrate those who attempt to do so.

Beer, S, *Heart of the Enterprise*. Chichester: Wiley, 1979. This describes Beer's viable system model, a topic not covered in this pamphlet but regarded by many as essential to understanding organisational performance. Beer's work is based in the tradition of engineering systems.

Capra, F, *The Web of Life*. London: Harper Collins, 1996. This book provides a comprehensive introduction to the ways in which systems thinking, chaos theory, complexity, self-organisation and evolution form a comprehensive and new view about the biology of life and how we come to know what we know. It is a valuable complement to the ideas set out in the present work.

Checkland, P and Scholes, J, *Soft Systems Methodology in Action*. Chichester: Wiley, 1990. This describes the mature version of SSM in some detail. The book also contains in-depth case studies on its application to public policy and commercial organisations. It complements the discussion of SSM in this pamphlet.

Forrester, JW, *Industrial Dynamics*. Cambridge MA: Wright-Allen Press, 1961. This is the book that established the field that became known as 'systems dynamics'. It explains the basics of stock and flow models and how they apply to industrial processes. Later, the same approach was used by the world modelling team responsible for *Limits to Growth*.

Schön, DA and Rein, M, *Frame Reflection: Towards the resolution of intractable policy controversies*. New York: Basic Books, 1994. This book explains how policy controversies become locked into mutually incompatible frameworks (modes of interpreting the world). The authors argue that the resolution of such controversies requires the creation of a meta-frame, generated by going up a level of abstraction. Schön has long been a leading systems thinker.

Verma, N, *Similarities, Connections and Systems: The search for a new rationality for planning and management*. Maryland: Lexington Books, 1998. This book focuses on the need for comprehensiveness in the planning and management professions, and leans heavily on systems thinking. It also proposes a pragmatic methodology, based on the work of William James, which aims to integrate sentiments and emotions in a rational framework.

Vickers, G, *The Art of Judgement: A study of policy making*. London: Chapman and Hall, 1965 (republished by Harper and Row, 1984). This

represents Vickers's original account
of the social process as 'an
appreciative system' and emphasises
the importance of judgement and
values in policy making.

Learning Resources

Educational resources in the United Kingdom are available through the principal university systems departments. These can be accessed through the following web sites:

Open University Systems	http://systems.open.ac.uk/page.cfm
Open University BBC courses	http://www.open2.net/systems/
University of Lancaster, Management Science Department	http://www.lums.lancs.ac.uk/mansci/
University of Hull	http://www.hull.ac.uk/hubs/research/groups/css/index.htm

The courses and materials from the Open University are the most accessible, being designed for distance learning. For further information, access the Open University web site on courses (**http://www3.open.ac.uk/courses/**) and look at the following courses:

Managing complexity: A systems approach (T306)

Systems thinking: Principles and practice (T205)

Experiencing systems (TXR 248)

Environmental decision making. A systems approach (T860)

Environmental ethics (T861)

Enterprise and the environment (T862)

Systems thinking and practice: A primer. (T551)

Systems thinking and practice: Diagramming (T552)

Systems thinking and practice: Modelling (T553)

Further information on systems thinking and soft systems methodology can be found through the following web sites:

Soft systems methodology on the Web	http://members.tripod.com/SSM_Delphi/ssm4.html
Systems thinking as applied to organisations	http://www.mapnp.org/library/systems/systems.htm
Systems thinking books	http://www.systemsthinkingpress.com/
Systems thinking and its relation to systems dynamics	http://www.albany.edu/cpr/sds/

For information on systems dynamics and its applications see the websites below:

Systems Dynamics Group at MIT	**http://sysdyn.mit.edu/sd-group/home.html**
Systems dynamics and systems	**http://www.uni-klu.ac.at/**
thinking list of links	**users/gossimit/links/bookmksd.htm**

Many websites describe systems ideas and their application to organisational and practical problems. These can be found using a standard search engine (such as **http://www.google.com**) and searching on key words such as 'systems thinking', 'soft systems', 'systems dynamics' and so on.